HOW TO ARRANGE FLOWERS

A Japanese Approach to English Design

HOW TO ARRANGE FLOWERS

A Japanese Approach
to English Design

TAEKO MARVELLY

Guild of Master Craftsman Publications Ltd

First published 2000 by

Guild of Master Craftsman Publications Ltd,

166 High Street, Lewes, East Sussex BN7 1XU

Reprinted 2002
Text and photographs © Taeko Marvelly 2000

© in the work, Guild of Master Craftsman Publications Ltd

ISBN 1 86108 152 9

Photography and cover photograph by Derek Cattani

Illustrations by Simon Rodway

Cover design by Amber Stoddart,
Guild of Master Craftsman Studio

Design by Angela Neal
Typeface: Futura

Colour origination by Viscan Graphics (Singapore)

Printed and bound in China by Sun Fung Offset Binding Company Limited.

To all my wonderful students
whose passionate engagement with flower arranging affirms my
belief that flowers have the power to transcend the boundaries of
communication around the world.

Also, to my two special daughters Hannah and Naomi for their
enthusiasm and support over the years.

CONTENTS

INTRODUCTION

Both the East and the West have long and vibrant traditions of flower arranging, developed out of distinct local customs and influences. In today's global culture, however, these diverse styles have 'fused' together to their mutual enrichment. The purpose of this book is to demonstrate my personal approach to this exciting, continually evolving art form.

RIGHT: *Star shape vertical. This arrangement has a very striking shape*

LEFT: *The Diagonal display is one of my more colourful abstract designs*

BELOW: *This arrangement is a variation on the rustic Country garden basket design*

Flowers are as fundamental to my life as breathing. Ever since I can remember they have helped shape my vision of the world and opened up endless opportunities for growth, both personally and professionally. I continue to be surprised by the ways in which flowers have the ability to delight and inspire with their infinite variety of colour, shape, texture and scent, and how the most simple arrangement can absolutely redefine an ordinary room. And therein lies the beauty of flower arranging: in its purest sense, it is the art of bringing nature (or at least the garden) into our interiors, whether it be our home, the office, or the venue for a special event, to brighten and inspire our everyday lives.

It is with this key concept of purity and simplicity in mind that I present the beginner and more competent arranger alike with my unique style of flower arranging. My work has been greatly influenced by three very different styles which have been borne of time spent studying, travelling and working in Japan, England and in Europe. These styles might be described as modern English, Continental and Japanese, or more precisely, Ikebana. As you work through the book, I hope that you gain a sense of the space and balance in the arrangements which is a unique feature of my personal style. The Ikebana principle encourages the arranger to display the flowers in a natural, yet

apparently random order, using the variety of flower faces and foliage to give depth and harmony, which balances well with the Western flair for freedom of design and interpretation. Aside from these formal influences, the designs reflect other, less tangible ones. As you will find with your own arrangements, something of one's own experiences and personality also make an impact on your displays.

In the following project chapters, I have selected those floral arrangements which have

been produced again and again over the years with great success, contributing to the ambience and enjoyment of many special occasions. They range in complexity, from the very simple but pleasing Round arrangement to the more complicated and striking Hogarth display, therefore I am confident you will have plenty of designs on which to practise your skills. It will take you relatively little time to produce arrangements of which you can be very proud, and with each new project you create, the more confidence you gain, enabling you to raise your skills to greater heights.

Finally, have fun with your materials and remember, there are never any mistakes, only experiments. Happy arranging!

ABOVE: *The Fan display can be adapted to almost any location*

RIGHT: *The Clover design beautifully combines both Japanese and Western influences*

BELOW LEFT: *The Rectangle arrangement*

PART ONE
Getting Started

GLOSSARY OF TERMS AND PLANT NAMES

In any book on flower arranging you will find discrepancies in the names given for flowers and foliage. This is quite common because some are known primarily by their Latin name, while others are known by their common name, and these might vary from country to country, and even person to person. To help you avoid confusion when buying from your florist or supplier, I include here alternative names that exist for flowers and foliage. As a general rule in this book, however, I have used the name most commonly used for a flower in English.

GLOSSARY OF TERMS

BACKING The rear face of the arrangement which disguises the floral foam base.

BLADE The flattened and normally broad part of a leaf.

BELOW: *Greening forms the first stage of any floral arrangement*

BLOOM A flower or blossom.

COLOUR BANDING A technique for distributing flowers in an even, yet apparently random, way into floral arrangements.

COLOUR GRADUATION A technique of arranging flowers which makes use of different tones of the same colour to create a more dramatic effect.

FLOWER HEAD A mass of small florets of petals that group together as one at the top of the stem of the flower.

GREENING The first stage of a floral arrangement, whereby the greenery is inserted into the display.

LINE FLOWER Flowers which are tall and narrow in character and used to add height and drama to floral arrangements.

MAIN FLOWER The most dominant flower in the arrangement, the purpose of which is to influence the overall shape.

ABOVE: *This display makes use of ivy, willow and many line flowers*

MAIN LINE The first and dominant line of an arrangement which structures the whole display.

MASS FLOWER Flowers which have large, round, bold flower heads, used to create impact in floral arrangements.

OUTLINE The outer lines which dictate the shape of the display.

POINTED FLOWER The shorter version of a line flower, more pointed in character and having a fuller stem of blooms.

POT-ET-FLEUR A style of flower arranging developed during the 1960s which utilizes pots and troughs of flowers to create a romantic, miniature garden display.

ROUND FLOWER Flowers which have round, bold heads, used to create impact.

GLOSSARY OF PLANT NAMES

Aconitum	Monkshood
Allium	Onion
Amaranthus	Cat's tail/Love lies bleeding
Anthurium	Flamingo flower/Painter's palette
Antirrhinum	Snapdragon
Aster	September Daisy
Astilbe	False goat's beard
Calistemon	Bottlebrush
Calla, or Arum lily	Zantedeschia
Carnation	Dianthus
Celosia	Cocks comb
China Aster	Callistephus
Chrysanthemum	Dendranthema
Crocosmia	Montbretia
Eryngium	Sea holly
Fennel	Feoniculum vulgare
Gypsophila	Baby's breath
Hypericum	St. John's Wort
Larkspur	Delphinium
Leatherleaf, or Fern	Chamaedaphne calyculata
Leucadendrum	Red Sunset
Liatris	Button snakeroot
Lily	Lilium
Limonium	Sea lavender
Mini Gerbera	Transvaal Daisy
Murtille	Myrtle or Myrtus
Ornithogalum	Star of Bethlehem
Polygonum	Snake wood
Rose	Rosa
Scabiosa	Scabious
Sedum	Stonecrop
Solidago	Golden rod
Statice	Psylliostachys
Sunflower	Helianthus
Trachelium	Blue throatwort
Tulip	Tulipa
Viburnum	Viburnum Tinus
Viburnum Opulus	Snowball

MATERIALS AND EQUIPMENT

To begin with, you require only a few inexpensive basic items in order to have everything you need for the arrangements featured in this book – although with repeated use you will find that they soon become invaluable! In time, once you have some experience, you may wish to purchase better quality equipment and extend your range of materials.

1 FLORAL FOAM

Floral foam is sometimes known by its more common brand name, Oasis®. Before you use the foam, you need to soak it in water. It cannot be used twice, so remember to cut it prior to immersion. Place the foam into a deep container more than double its size, then fill it with water and leave to soak. Allow the foam to totally immerse itself at its own pace, releasing all the air from inside. If the foam is forced underwater, it will retain air and prove less effective. Foam should not be soaked twice as this also reduces its effectiveness.

Floral foam is available in a variety of shapes and sizes, the rectangular and cylindrical shapes being the most popular. When I refer to floral foam in the project chapters, I mean the wet variety. You should never use the dry variety of floral foam when working with fresh flowers – they will lack moisture and fade quickly.

2 FLORAL FOAM HOLDERS

Floral foam holders are more commonly known as frogs. Essentially, the frog is used in conjunction with floral foam fix to stick the foam to the container to hold the arrangement steady.

3 CANDLE HOLDER

If you wish to add a candle or two to your arrangement, a candle holder can be inserted into the foam base, providing excellent support. If the candle is particularly large or unwieldy then a little floral fix can be added to the base of the candle to provide additional strength.

4 TURNTABLE

Turntables are extremely helpful for viewing your arrangement, allowing you to judge the balance of your display as you work. They are also very easy to use: simply place your arrangement onto the turntable and you are ready to work.

5 FLORAL FIX

Floral fix is a type of adhesive putty used specifically for floristry, stronger than Blu-tack, which is used to fix all containers, holders and other materials together, but particularly for fixing the container to the display surface.

6 FLORAL FOAM TAPE

An adhesive tape used in addition to the floral holder to secure the foam to your container and to provide greater support. Always 'pinch' the tape to halve its width as it crosses over the top face of the foam. This will ensure maximum room is given to the flower stems.

7 FLORAL TAPE

Floral tape is sometimes known as Gutta tape and is used to camouflage the steel wire used in some arrangements. Floral tape is widely available in two varieties: paper or plastic.

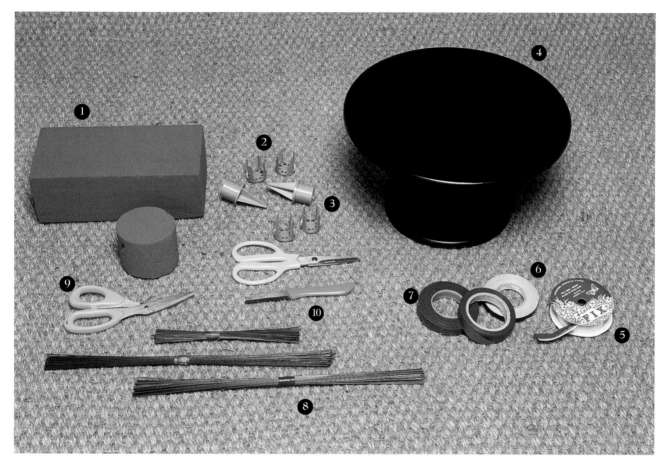

8 CUT WIRE

Cut wire is also known as stub wire. There are many different gauges of floral wire and these are used to support weak stems and help shape the direction of the flower and foliage. Even after wrapping in floral tape, it is advisable to make only limited use of it to preserve the natural shape of the flowers.

9 SCISSORS

It is worth keeping two different types of scissors: one pair to cut fresh flowers, foliage and wire and the other to cut ribbon, cellophane and paper.

10 KNIFE

A sharp knife is one of the most essential pieces of equipment in the floral arranger's kit. It is best to cut fresh flowers and foliage with a knife because it creates less damage to the central artery, thereby aiding its ability to soak up moisture once inserted into an arrangement. A knife is also useful for other general tasks, for example removing thorns, sharpening the end of tough or thick-stemmed flowers and foliage, and removing what I term 'knuckles' from flower stems. When cutting them, always remember to do so at an oblique angle.

ABOVE: *A selection of the most essential materials and equipment for flower arranging*

WHICH CONTAINER?

It is sometimes difficult to decide which container is best for a particular arrangement. In the following tables I provide suggestions for matching your vessel to your display. The recommended containers approximate the ones I use in the project chapters. You can try different vessels to see which work well for you, keeping in mind the overall presentation of your arrangement.

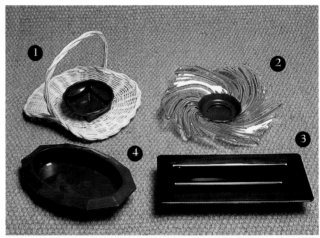

Type of container	Suitable arrangements
1 Urn	Hogarth, Narrow triangle, Clover, Asymmetrical triangle, S shape, Diagonal
2 Roman vase	Triangle, Round, Oval, L shape, Cone shape, Fan shape
3 Arabian vase	Clover, Triangle, Narrow triangle, Asymmetrical triangle, Hogarth, Diagonal
4 Classic bowl	Round, Triangle, L shape, Cone shape, Fan shape
5 Large London bowl	Fan shape, Triangle, Crescent, L shape, Rectangle, triangle, Hogarth, Diagonal

Type of container	Suitable arrangements
1 Basket and plastic dish	Country garden basket, Round, Oval
2 Crystal dish and plastic dish	Cone shape, Star shape vertical, Round, Triangle, L shape, Crescent table centre, Fan shape
3 Rectangle plastic dish	Rectangle, Oval, Triangle, Crescent, L shape table centre, Fan shape
4 Oval plastic dish	L shape, Crescent, Oval, Fan shape, Crescent table centre, L shape table centre, Triangle, Rectangle

Type of container	Suitable arrangements
1 Candle stand with candle cup attachment	Diagonal, Round, Oval, Narrow triangle, Clover, Asymmetrical triangle, S shape
2 Figurine	S shape, Narrow triangle, Clover, Asymmetrical triangle, Hogarth, Diagonal
3 Greek-style vase	Oval, Triangle, Crescent, L shape, Fan shape
4 Small London bowl	Triangle, Crescent, L shape Fan shape
5 Terracotta pot	Round, Triangle, L shape, Cone shape, Fan shape

Type of container	Suitable arrangements
1 Terracotta pot	Asymmetrical triangle, Triangle, Narrow triangle, Clover, Hogarth, Cone shape, Diagonal
2 Wrought iron S stand (black)	Narrow triangle, Triangle, Clover, Asymmetrical triangle, S shape, Diagonal
3 Wrought iron S stand (verdigris)	Narrow triangle, Triangle, Clover, Asymmetrical triangle, S shape, Diagonal
4 Ornate brass vase	Crescent, Oval, Triangle, L shape, Fan shape

SELECTING THE RIGHT CONTAINER FOR YOUR ARRANGEMENT

Of prime importance when selecting the right container is the location for the arrangement. After that, you need to decide the overall height, width and depth of the arrangement, and how large a reservoir of water you require. You should also consider whether you wish your container to be visible, a part of the display itself, or whether you would prefer it to be hidden. Finally, you may need to consider its weight and balance in addition to the aesthetic value of your arrangement, particularly if it is one intended for a special event.

Once you have decided which container you require, you need to consider how you will keep your arrangement moist. Fix the floral foam to its base, ensuring that the foam is saturated with water, is securely taped to the container, that sufficient space is left to create a reservoir and that access is available after the arrangement is completed to allow space for watering.

GENERAL TIPS FOR FLOWER ARRANGING

For many students of flower arranging, or flower arrangers themselves, there are a number of factors to take into consideration before you select the most appropriate arrangement for your purpose. You also need to know how to prepare and maintain it for maximum impact and longevity. In this section I take you through how to select your foliage, prepare your flowers and container and the assembly of the arrangement itself. Once you have followed these guidelines a few times, you will be able to approach your flower arranging projects with confidence and create really special displays for the home, for family and friends, and perhaps in time, if you wish, professional commissions.

WHAT IS THE PURPOSE OF YOUR ARRANGEMENT?

Floral arrangements are popular for all sorts of occasions and are always greatly appreciated. Before you do anything else, begin by asking yourself the following key question: what is the purpose of the arrangement you wish to create? This is, I hope, the easiest question to answer and should fall into one of the following categories: a party, a present, a special occasion, for use in the home or for commercial use in an office or foyer. Perhaps you are planning a dinner party, or would like to arrange something for a house-warming gift, or more elaborately still, have been asked to dress a church or hall for a wedding ceremony.

SELECTING YOUR FLOWERS AND FOLIAGE

Once you have established the purpose of the arrangement, you must decide what kind of arrangement you wish to create, what kind of flowers and foliage you require, which container is most suitable for displaying your arrangement and, importantly, the location for the arrangement once it is complete. You should consider the following key factors:

❧ If, for example, the arrangement is to be a gift for someone, what is the reason for the present – a thank you, birthday or other special event?

RIGHT: *The Narrow Triangle arrangement is particularly suitable for galleried halls and other grand spaces*

BELOW: *Here I am demonstrating a Clover arrangement to my students*

ABOVE: *A selection of flowers from The Daisy Chain. Always buy the freshest flowers that are available*

ABOVE RIGHT: *Choose the most appropriate flowers and foliage for your arrangement – but remember to have fun with them, too*

Is there a seasonal impact to be considered? How will you deliver the arrangement when it is finished? Answering these questions will help you decide the most appropriate colours, scents, size of flowers, etc.

❧ Where will your arrangement be displayed? You should make yourself aware of the environment in which the arrangement will be displayed because this will influence your choice of flowers and foliage. Is it for a home, an event, or an office? What kind of room or building are you creating the arrangement for? What kind of period style does it have: Victorian, Edwardian, modern, contemporary? What colour scheme, décor, curtains, carpet, etc. does it have? You should also consider the overall texture of the location in question. Your choice of flowers and foliage should reflect the environment, whether it is heavy and dark, or light and airy. Do not forget to consider the atmospheric conditions, too, for example, air-conditioning. Is the location draughty, still, hot, cool or subject to changes in temperature which might affect the

display? Remember, too, your location needs to be accessible not simply for viewing, but for watering, too.

❧ The type and amount of lighting available for your location is another factor to consider. The ambient lighting pattern will have a bearing on your selection, too. Your location might have mostly artificial light, natural daylight, diffused lighting, focused lighting, subdued lighting – and each requires a different approach to colour and texture.

❧ Once you have established the above, you can decide the range and size of flowers and foliage you require. Your location might well dictate how large and bold your flowers can be. After all, you want to enhance the location, not overwhelm it. Perhaps the location is very intimate, in which case you might prefer to use smaller, more delicate shapes and shades of flowers. In general, however, you will need to consider larger flowers to provide the focus for the arrangement, medium-headed flowers for the outline, and smaller flowers to create rhythm and movement to the overall arrangement.

In the projects which follow, I have selected specific varieties and colours of flowers and foliage which I feel work well for the design, but please feel free to experiment with them. My designs are influenced by colour, texture and form. If you wish to substitute a flower, simply select another with a similar or complementary colour and form.

HOW TO PREPARE YOUR FLOWERS AND FOLIAGE

Before you begin your flower arrangement, there are a few housekeeping chores to do and pieces of advice to keep in mind.

- It is always worth buying the best quality flowers and foliage you can afford, and preferably from a good supplier with whom you can build a relationship. Good quality flowers may seem an extravagance, but they are fresh, in premium condition and will last much longer than their cheaper counterparts, which makes them a good buy. Cheap flowers bought at the roadside or from a draughty shopfront are fine if intended to last only a short time, but for flower arranging cannot generally sustain themselves for very long.

- The first thing to do when you prepare your materials and equipment is to ensure that everything is bacteria-free. The healthy maintenance of the flowers and foliage in the arrangement will ensure the display's longevity. Take some bleach and a little water and make up a mild solution to rinse clean all buckets, vases and containers you intend to use.

- To ensure the health of your flowers and foliage when preparing the stems, I recommend that you do two things: firstly, remove all thorns, excess leaves and any surface knots that may be on the stems, but avoid tearing the skin of the stems as this will encourage bacteria and allow germs into the flower. Next, cut the stem cleanly with a knife below the water line. This may seem a strange thing to do, but it increases the flower's ability to take in water. It also lessens the damage done to the flower's central artery.

- I recommend that you use flower food additives to lengthen the life span of your flowers. Once you have made up the original solution of clean water and additive, you should top up the water level in your arrangement with more clean water, or further solution. If you use water only, ensure that you change it regularly rather than topping it up with fresh water which allows the build up of decaying leaves under the surface of the water which poisons the water reservoir.

- A common problem for flowers is their tendency to droop. A special technique for restoring roses to their alert state is to straighten and then wrap

BELOW: *The S shape arrangement can be adapted to form a dramatic table centre display*

the full length of the flower stems together tightly as a bunch, cleanly cutting the ends and immersing the stems into boiling hot water for anything between three to six minutes. Then remove and soak in cold water for approximately two to three hours which enables the flowers to drink water. This method is very effective because it shocks the flower's system back into life.

HOW TO ASSEMBLE YOUR ARRANGEMENT

The ideal spot to create your arrangement is the intended location of the display. Although it might seem easier to arrange the display in your own home or place of business and then transport it to your location, you risk damaging the precious flowers and foliage en route for which you will never forgive yourself – and if it is a commission, neither will your client! If you can organize it, it is safer to assemble the whole arrangement on site. It also guarantees that your materials remain fresh until the very last moment. Once on site, make sure that you keep the flowers in water, close to hand, so that they can be transferred directly from water and inserted into the foam without delay. These conditions are preferable and may not always be available, so do be prepared to include the transportation of your arrangement into your planning if necessary.

HOW TO USE FLOWER FOAM

To prepare your stem for insertion into the flower foam, allow up to 10cm (4in) of straight, stripped stem, removing all thorns, knuckles and leaves, and sharpen the root end to be inserted into the foam. This creates a pointed spear shaft which will lessen the size of the hole in the foam created by the stem. When inserting the flower stem or foliage push in only approximately 3cm (1¼) in order to create a nice, soft effect when the arrangement is complete. To disguise these areas of the foam base, use stems of greenery to do the greening at the end.

It is usual to use all five faces of your foam base when working an arrangement.

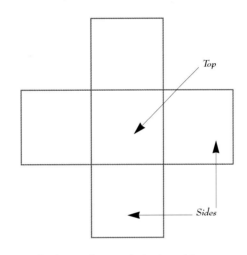

ABOVE: *This diagram illustrates the five faces of the arrangement. It is a uniform feature throughout the book to show you where to insert greenery in the early stages of each arrangement.*

However, when inserting your stems into the arrangement, be careful to remember the following:

- to vary the direction of your insertions to avoid creating a fracture point within the foam.
- to ensure that the stems do not drink water from the same point, thereby drying out the foam too quickly.

A word of warning – always be careful where you place your floral foam base once it has been soaked because it has a tendency to stain surfaces and display dishes. If, therefore, you wish to use a particularly special display dish for your arrangement, it is advisable to insert the foam into a plastic dish first to protect it.

CREATING THE OUTLINE

Greenery is used to create the outline or boundaries of flower arrangements. It effectively fixes the main meridians, east to west and north to south, and thereby sets up the structure of the arrangement. Complete this structure before any flowers are arranged into the display. Greenery is also used to disguise the foam base, which detracts from the arrangement itself. It provides excellent background colour and textures for the rest of the flowers, too. Before you begin your outline, select your greenery. I often use Italian ruscus and leatherleaf which work well together, but there are other kinds of beautiful greenery, for example pittosporum, and it is always nice to offer a variety of textures in an arrangement.

HOW TO ARRANGE YOUR FLOWERS

I always approach my flower arrangements in the same way – it is often best to be methodical. Once

the greenery is in place, begin to create what is known as 'colour banding'. Insert the medium-sized flowers to create a single band of colour across the arrangement, followed by a second, opposite band of a different variety of flower. Work these bands from opposite top corners, across each other, to their diagonally opposite base corners – although quite often they do not need to be perfectly centred, nor follow a straight line. These bands form the second layer of the arrangement.

Once completed, you can insert the key flowers into the arrangement. These flowers really form the focal point of the arrangement. Insert individual heads in a zigzag pattern through the body of the arrangement to emphasize the shape of the arrangement. You can use as many as five or six heads, or more, depending on the size of the display. Finally, insert the detail flowers effectively to give the arrangement depth, as well as fill in any gaps which might have been left. The detail flowers also give the display a sense of movement and balance. At this point, take care to ensure that you do not forget the sides, back and bottom of the arrangement. All flower arrangements are viewed in the round, with the exception of those intended to back against a wall, and each aspect should appear to be nicely balanced, without being over-crowded. In their natural environment, flowers grow to different lengths and this should be reflected in your arrangement. You need to place the flowers as though at random, but in actual fact, the technique involves placing the flowers along what I call an 'outline in the air'. By this I mean you should place each bloom facing outwards at an invisible line running from the top to the bottom of any given length of the arrangement.

A good general point to remember when creating your arrangement is that too many flowers can destroy impact. Each flower head should have plenty of room around it in order to stand out against the frame of greenery which serves to highlight its individual character. The arrangement truly works when you are able to appreciate the key elements and the overall effect at the same time. This approach to floral design is inspired by my Ikebana training, which has had a profound influence on my arranging techniques generally, and on this book in particular.

THE FINAL VIEWING

Your final task is to view the arrangement from all sides. If you use a turntable you can manoeuvre it until you are happy with every aspect. Alternatively, walk around the arrangement and view it from every angle. Perhaps the most important is the side view. Many students forget to check the arrangement from this side which can result in an unbalanced display. Remember, an arrangement is not viewed solely from

ABOVE: *The completed arrangement. Enjoy the moment!*

the front. Check also that there is no foam visible and that the backing is satisfactorily filled in. If you step back a few paces, you will gain a different perspective, enabling you to appreciate the overall effect. Check the level of water in the container, lightly mist the arrangement with fresh water to create a glistening effect and clear the area of debris. Now look away from the arrangement and then refocus your attention on it so that you see it with a fresh eye. If you feel that it is complete, enjoy the moment. It is a real pleasure to look upon something beautiful that is alive and the culmination of your own efforts.

PART TWO

Circular Arrangements

Flowers and Greenery

- (1) Bupleurum or gypsophila

- (2) Spray roses (Joy)

- (3) Italian ruscus

- (4) China asters

- (5) Spray carnations

- (6) Leatherleaf

Materials and Equipment

- Decorative display dish (I use one with legs for extra height)

- Floral foam brick

- Plastic dish

- Floral tape

- Sharp floristry knife or scissors

- Optional items: candle, ribbons and fruit for decoration

ROUND

This is a very popular arrangement with both students and clients around the world. It is relatively simple to achieve, but its very simplicity creates real impact as a table centre decoration.

METHOD

1 Wet one third of a floral foam brick and place it in a plastic dish. Take some floral tape and discreetly secure the foam to the dish. Place the plastic dish in a decorative display dish. Once in place, you should be able to see approximately 3–4cm (1½in) of foam above its rim. To avoid the risk of staining or damaging your display dish always ensure that you put the foam in the plastic dish first. If the arrangement is to be used as a centre table decoration, you might like to use a silver tureen or a salad bowl, both of which lend a very elegant look to the table.

2 You are now ready to begin the arrangement itself. The primary consideration in relation to the size of your display is the size of your table. For a round table, the outline of flowers should ideally be within one-third of its diameter and the height of the arrangement should fall below the eye-line of your guests to ensure that they can see each other when

seated! Once you have determined these factors, you can assess the length and size of your outline shape and the size and quantity of flowers to be used.

To create an outline, take five stems of Italian ruscus and cut them to length. Insert each into the sides of the foam to form a five-pointed star shape, ensuring that the

angle between each stem is consistent. Cut a further stem to one-third of the size of the previous five stems and insert into the centre of the foam.

3 Continue to create a circular outline with the Italian ruscus and leatherleaf; this is commonly known as 'greening'. Insert the flat leatherleaf into the foam, varying the angles slightly to create a feeling of movement within the design. When you have completed the outline, disguise the foam base with some greenery. As you work, remember to check the arrangement in the round, including the top, to ensure that you have a consistent, balanced piece.

4 You are now ready to add the spray carnations. Cut each to the appropriate height and, following a zigzag formation, insert them into the foam in the diagonal band shown in the photo. This is known as colour banding. Use the sprays still in bud with longer stems to create the outline and the flowers in bloom with shorter stems to fill the centre of the display. By arranging the flowers in this systematic way you ensure that you achieve balance

and movement in the arrangement. Put a few of the carnation sprays to one side in case you need to till a few gaps later on, to finish off your arrangement.

5 Now turn to the China asters. Insert them into their own diagonal band, again using the flowers still in bud to create an outline and the flowers in bloom to fill the centre of the display. At this stage, take a look at the arrangement from the top to check that the flowers in the centre are completely straight and vertical and that those nearer the edges angle slight

outwards. From a side view, check that your flowers are positioned horizontally, with those nearest to the rim of the dish angled downwards. Overall, the arrangement should present as a flowing sequence of angled flowers, each enjoying room to breathe, yet contributing to a greater, cohesive whole. This characteristic is known as the 'English' style.

6 Cut the spray roses to give them maximum length. Insert them judiciously throughout the arrangement,

rather than into a diagonal band as you have with the spray carnations, ensuring that you maintain their height throughout. Again, always keep in mind a sense of balance and movement. Take a look at your arrangement from the top and the sides to check that it has a nice shape.

7 The final floral addition to any flower arrangement is normally also the smallest and requires a fine sense of judgement. Use these tiny, delicate blooms to achieve the following effect: to 'lift' and soften the diverse mix of stems already inserted into the arrangement. Gypsophila is often utilized in this way with great success. As always, do not be tempted to overwork this part of the arrangement, or it will simply look too

fussy. Subtlety is key here. For this arrangement I use bupleurum which is a member of the Euphorbia family. There is only one disadvantage with bupleurum and that is its tendency to secrete a white substance when its stem is cut. To help coagulate this secretion, and to extend its flowering period, place the stems in hot water for a few minutes immediately after cutting, after which they should revive.

FURTHER IDEAS

If you wish to elaborate on the arrangement further, perhaps for a special dinner, why not add a colour co-ordinated candle to the centre of the display. For a very different, natural look, create a display with fruit and ribbons, which will infuse your home with a beautiful fragrance. For this arrangement, create another round shape, but use fruit from the garden and display them in a terracotta pot. Use any excess fruit you have, however misshapened, to add to the interest of the display. Before you begin, give the fruit and leaves a good polish with either a house plant polish or egg white diluted with water. Use gold wire, either straight or curled in a 'telephone cable' style, to add to the opulence of the arrangement. Disguise the bottom of your arrangement with bun moss. If you wish, use fruits of a lighter hue, for example lemons with white grapes, in combination with variegated ivy, to create a fresh, spring-like ambience.

Flowers and Greenery

- ❦ (1) Amaranthus
- ❦ (2) Scabiosa
- ❦ (3) Spray carnations
- ❦ (4) Lilies (American)
- ❦ (5) Hypericum
- ❦ (6) Tulips (Pink Diamond)
- ❦ (7) Palm leaves
- ❦ (8) Italian ruscus

Materials and Equipment

- ❦ Tall, Greek-style china display dish
- ❦ Floral foam brick
- ❦ Floral tape
- ❦ Sharp floristry knife or scissors

OVAL

The oval arrangement makes a very pleasant table centre display for the home, but can also be adapted to suit a more formal occasion, perhaps a wedding or a business conference.

❶

METHOD

1 Wet one half of a foam brick and, using floral tape, secure it to your chosen dish. I use a Greek urn-style china display dish for this arrangement, but you can use any similar china or plastic dish. To begin, create the outline of the display with some small palm leaves. Insert the first four stems into the foam along the edge of the dish and the final stem in the centre of the foam.

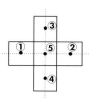

2 Now turn to the greening. Take some Italian ruscus and create an oval-shaped outline with the stems. The rotundity of your oval will depend upon where you insert the long stems of greenery into the foam. For example, the oval shape will appear slimmer if they are inserted close to both sides of 1 and 2, and more squat if the stems are inserted into each corner of the foam. Angle the leaves to emphasize the shape and create an impression of movement. Once completed, check to see how the arrangement looks from the top. The flowers in the centre should be vertical and those near the edges should be angled. From the sides, check that the flowers are horizontal and those nearest to the rim

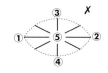

2a

2b

angled downwards.
Finally, disguise the
foam base with some greenery.

3 Taking the spray carnations, create
a strong diagonal band of colour,
moving from the back left of the
arrangement to the front right. Use flowers
in bud with longer stems to create the
outline itself and
flowers in bloom
with shorter stems to

fill the centre of the display. Following the diagram, you can emphasize the oval shape of the arrangement further if you insert the longer stems next to 1 and 2. To add height, insert a large, open carnation at 5.

4 Taking the pink tulips, create a second diagonal band of colour. Cut each stem to an individual length for a natural look and to create a feeling of space within the design. Tulips have large leaves which tend to bend easily, therefore I recommend that you remove them, with the exception of a few small ones near to the flower head. Additionally, wash off any dirt gathered around the leaves and stem which might encourage bacteria. Tulips also have a tendency to grow towards the light which can distort the outline. To prevent this, pierce a small hole the size of a pin into each stem, directly under the flower head. If you wish, arrange the tulips a little higher than the outline, but only by the flower head itself or the arrangement will appear overbalanced.

5 The main flower in the arrangement is the lily. I use dusky pink American lilies which provide a bold splash of colour to the arrangement, but if you cannot find them or find another that you prefer, you can

substitute them for another variety. Use flowers in bud with longer stems to create an outline and flowers in bloom with shorter stems to fill the centre of the group. To encourage your lilies to bloom for a little longer, remove as much of the excess pollen as possible, making sure that you handle the delicate petals with care. If you have one, an artist's paintbrush is useful for this task.

6 To finish off the display, turn to the amaranthus, scabiosa and hypericum, and arrange them. These flowers work very well together and add a beautiful soft, natural feel to the arrangement as well as creating balance and movement. Amaranthus flowers are a striking wine red in colour and have a naturally curved shape which is very appealing. Insert the amaranthus and scabiosa judiciously into the arrangement, ensuring that they do not project beyond the outline. Finally, fill in any gaps with hypericum, making sure it is distributed evenly throughout.

7 Check the overall shape and the balance of the flowers by turning the arrangement around on the turntable to view from all angles. Alternatively, walk around the display itself. Make any adjustments that you feel are necessary. Your arrangement is now complete.

FURTHER IDEAS

If you wish to vary the oval arrangement, you might like to try using a shallow dish, adapting the flowers nearest to the rim so that they just barely brush the table. You can also experiment with the types of flowers you use which will, in turn, govern the height of your final display. To create a floral arrangement on a flat surface, for example a piano (see left), table edge or top table centre display for a wedding, use a plastic tray to protect your surface against damage from the wet foam block. Introduce the trailing greenery in the early stages and insert them at the front half of the arrangement only. Arrange the flowers for the back half and the remainder of the arrangement in precisely the same way as described above, inserting some blooms lower on the leading rear edge to give the display a better sense of balance.

PART THREE

Triangular
Arrangements

Flowers and Greenery

- ❦ (1) Lisianthus
- ❦ (2) Spray carnations
- ❦ (3) Leatherleaf
- ❦ (4) Bupleurum
- ❦ (5) Lily (Star Gazer)
- ❦ (6) Veronica
- ❦ (7) Pittosporum
- ❦ (8) Italian ruscus

Materials and Equipment

- ❦ Roman vase or other decorative dish
- ❦ Floral foam brick
- ❦ Floral tape
- ❦ Sharp scissors or knife

TRIANGLE

This is a beautifully symmetrical arrangement which will make a dramatic impact in any room and for any occasion. If you like, experiment with your selection of flowers, perhaps adapting them according to the season, to create a truly individual display.

METHOD

1 Wet half a foam brick and use floral tape to secure it to your chosen display dish. I use a Roman vase as a decorative dish but you can use any similar tall vessel. Once in place, you should be able to see approximately 3–4cm (1½in) of foam above its rim. Take some Italian ruscus and create the main arteries of the arrangement. Cut the first stem to a length which suits the location of the arrangement and the size of your vase and insert at 1, allowing it to angle gently backwards. Cut a further two stems to two-thirds the length of the first and insert them at either side of the vase, at 2 and 3, angling them downwards. Cut a further stem to one third of the length of your first and insert it at 4.

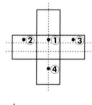

2 Now turn to the greening, using Italian ruscus, leatherleaf and pittosporum. Your aim is to create a flat, triangular back 'wall' for your arrangement. Take some of the Italian ruscus and leatherleaf and build up the triangle from 1 to 2 and 3. Take some

further stems and, following the shape of a bow, create another outline from 2 through 4 to 3. To avoid overloading the front of the display, angle the leaves at the wall slightly backwards. Additionally, to extend the width of the arrangement, create a longer outline between 1

and 4 to allow more room for flowers between them, and to create a better sense of movement. Taking the pittosporum, create a diagonal band of colour from the top left of the arrangement to the bottom right. If you prefer, you can use other types of greenery instead. Once completed, cover the foam with greenery.

3 Now add the spray carnations. Cut the stems to maximum length. Keeping within the outline formed by 1, 2, 3 and 4, and working a diagonall band of colour from top left to bottom right, place the flowers in bud with longer stems into the foam to build up the shape of the arrangement, then fill in the centre with the flowers in bloom with shorter stems. As you work, ensure that the flowers in the centre are vertical and that those near to the edges are angled. Remember to check the side view to ensure that those stems placed at the sides of the foam are horizontal, that those nearest to the rim of the dish are angled downwards and that those at the back are angled slightly outwards. If you

slightly alter the height of each of the carnations, this will emphasize the sense of depth and movement in the arrangement.

4 Take the stems of lisianthus and create another diagonal band of colour in the arrangement. You will, by now, be forming a lovely contrast between the ivory lisianthus and the very dark pink carnations. If, as in this instance, you have one colour which stands out more than another, be judicious in the amount you use of that colour in order to maintain a nice balance between the two of them.

5 The Star Gazer lily is the main flower in the arrangement. Take the stems and, following a zigzag formation, insert them into the foam. Try to keep the heads upright and facing frontwards, following the 'outline in the air', but do not allow the flower heads to fall too far forwards. I tend to use a lily with a longer stem on the front right of the arrangement and a larger flower with a shorter stem in the centre of the display to create a nice, open shape. As before, if you want to encourage your lilies to last longer, carefully remove the pollen from petals with an artist's brush or other soft medium. The best time to do this is when the flowers begin to open so that there is less risk of staining and damage to the delicate petals.

⑤

This is really a larger version of a triangle display and can be positioned either against a wall or as the centre piece on a table which can be viewed from every angle. The frames give a focal point to the arrangement and turn it into a 'living picture'. To create both the wall and the centre display make a four-sided box out of the picture frames and screw them together. Once completed, mount it around your floral display, being careful not to damage your precious flowers as you do so. If you want to do something really dramatic, arrange a different colour scheme, using different flowers, on each of the four faces of the arrangement.

6 Take some veronica and blend in with the lisianthus, the lilies and the carnations. The purple of the veronica balances the other two well here.

7 To finish, take some bupleurum and insert into the arrangement. The summery green of this flower beautifully enhances the established outline of greenery in the display. You can also use it judiciously to disguise the foam base. To do this, cut a few short stems and work them together in a mass, without overcrowding, until the foam is disguised. A feeling of space and movement is key to the success of the arrangement.

⑦

Flowers and Greenery

- (1) Rose (Jaguar)
- (2) Leatherleaf
- (3) Spray carnations
- (4) Statice
- (5) Celosia
- (6) Italian ruscus
- (7) Myriocladus

Materials and Equipment

- S-shape stand or other decorative display stand or dish
- Floral foam brick
- Floral tape
- Frog and floral fix
- Sharp scissors or knife

NARROW TRIANGLE

This second triangular arrangement follows a similar design to the first, but has a much more acute shape. It is particularly suitable for high-ceilinged rooms such as those found in churches or grand old houses with a galleried hall.

METHOD

1 For this arrangement I use a striking wrought iron S-shape stand instead of a conventional dish. Wet one third of a foam brick and secure it to the stand with floral tape. Once in place, you should be able to see approximately 3–4cm (1½in) of foam above its rim. Before cutting any flowers for the arrangement, consider its location, your display stand and the size of your flowers. Then, take a stem of Italian ruscus and insert it at 1. Ensure that the first stem is longer than usual, about twice the height of your display stand. To emphasize the naturally curved shape of the Italian ruscus, angle the stems slightly

backwards, like a
shallow bow, to
form the back 'wall'
of the arrangement.

Cut three further ruscus stems to one-third
of the length of the first stem. Insert these at
2, 3 and 4, using the natural curve to
angle them slightly downwards. This
shape forms the basic structure of the
arrangement.

2 Now work on the greening. Using
Italian ruscus and leatherleaf, make
a second, narrow triangular back wall
from 1 to 2 and 3. Working from 2
through 4 to 3 in a bow shape, create a
further outline with the stems. Cut shorter
stems of ruscus and insert them judiciously
to disguise the rim of the dish. Myriocladus
has lovely dense foliage; use it to fill in the

gaps rather than contribute to the outline of
the arrangement. Disguise the foam with
additional greenery.

3 Take the spray carnations and create
a diagonal band of colour within the
arrangement. To emphasize the tall, slim
character of this
arrangement, select those
carnations with a vivid
colour. Insert them from
top left to bottom right, altering the stem
length of each flower to add height and
depth to your arrangement. Ensure that you
keep the flower stems longer than the
Italian ruscus to emphasize the
arrangement's elegant shape. Check from
the top and side that the carnations in the
centre are vertical and that those near the
edge of the foam are angled forwards.

4 Take some statice and create a
second diagonal band of colour with
them. Statice is another spray-style flower,

so cut the stems to maximum length, ensuring that your cut is aimed just above a 'knuckle' in the stem. This encourages the stems to absorb water efficiently and also avoids creating unsightly holes in the foam. Put aside some statice in case you need to fill any gaps later, to finish the display.

5 Before you add the orange celosia to the arrangement, prepare the stems. Celosia stems are thick, so take a knife and pare down the bottom of each to avoid making unnecessarily large holes in the foam. In addition, because celosia leaves die off quickly, it is best to remove the leaves. Working in a zigzag formation, arrange the flowers. As you work, pay close attention to the overall balance of the arrangement. If you wish, you might like to try other similarly shaped line flowers;

delphinium, larkspur, gladiolus and stock would make fine alternatives to celosia.

6 Now arrange the roses. Red roses provide a wonderful contrast of shape and texture to the celosia and are the key flower in the arrangement. Place them following the same guidelines as above. The celosia and the roses are both vivid colours, so it is best to use one more prominently than the other to avoid clashing and to maintain a good sense of balance. If you feel the arrangement needs more flowers, add one or two until you are satisfied with the shape. Similarly, if you feel the arrangement is over-balanced, remove one or two. Sometimes it is better to remove one, because too many flowers risk loss of movement and shape. Once this has been completed, your arrangement will be finished.

FURTHER IDEAS

This style was made popular in the 1960s and remains a striking design today. It works particularly well in a

church or formal environment, but would look equally impressive in a corner of your own home. The wrought iron pedestal lends the arrangement a very grand look and is made complete by the judicious use of garden greenery and cascading trailing ivy. To add emphasis to this triangular arrangement, use plenty of willow and line flowers such as lupins, stocks or delphiniums.

Flowers and Greenery

- (1) Leatherleaf
- (2) Aconitum
- (3) Astilbe
- (4) Scabius
- (5) Lisianthus
- (6) Veronica
- (7) Italian ruscus

Materials and Equipment

- Arabian or other tall vase
- Floral foam brick
- Floral tape
- Sharp knife or scissors

CLOVER

This arrangement is inspired by the shape of the three-leaf clover. It has a three-pronged star shape encapsulated within a triangle and is most effectively displayed in a tall vase to accentuate its trailing curves.

METHOD

1 Wet one-third of a floral foam brick and use floral tape to secure it into the neck of an Arabian vase. Once in place, you should be able to see approximately 3–4cm (1½in) of foam above its rim. Now create the main outline of the arrangement, working from 1 to 4 on the diagram (right). Take some Italian ruscus and cut your first stem according to the desired location of the arrangement, or at least to 1½ times the height of your vase. Insert it at 1, angling it slightly backwards at the top. Cut two further stems to two-thirds of the length of the first and insert them at 2 and 3, curving them slightly downwards, but not too low or the clover shape will extend too far. Cut a final stem to one-quarter of the length of the first and insert at 4. You now have the basic structure for your arrangement.

2 Make a clover shape with the Italian ruscus and the leatherleaf. Cut the stems to half the length of the very first stem and insert them with a firm hand straight into the foam on both sides of the vertical artery at 1. Insert two further stems of the same length on either side of the artery between 2 and 3, positioning them

slightly forward and at a downward angle to form a bow-shaped front to the clover shape. Take a couple of shorter stems and insert them to create two inverted V shapes at the bottom. As you work, be careful to maintain the slim character of the arrangement as far as possible. Finally, disguise the foam base

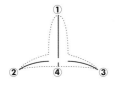

with a little greenery, preferably the bushy leaves of the Italian ruscus rather than the flat leatherleaf. Use leatherleaf, cut to half the length of the original stem, to disguise the back of the foam so that the arrangement can be viewed from every angle without revealing the foam base.

3 Next, take some lisianthus and work a diagonal band of colour from just left of the original upright stem across the arrangement to the bottom right. Lisianthus varies in shades of colour, so pay attention to this when inserting them into the foam; deeper shades of

colour should be cut short and positioned centrally to add definition and paler shades of longer stems along the outline to soften the edges. I use the purple lisianthus for this arrangement, but it is also available in pink, cream, white, in hybrid varieties and both single and double blooms.

4 As before, create a diagonal band of colour with the scabious. Scabious has a prominent round flower head which means that its stem remains visible. Cut the stems to slightly different lengths to stagger their appearance over the diagonal band and to avoid making the arrangement too heavy or one-sided. To disguise the stems themselves,

judiciously add some greenery. At this stage, put aside a few stems of flowers in bud in case you need to fill any gaps in the arrangement later on.

5 Aconitum is possibly the most prominent flower in the arrangement. In Britain, it is also known as monkshood, monkscap, helmet flower and wolf's bane due to its shape. It is a line flower, so be restrained when cutting it to emphasize its natural character, and then, working in a zigzag formation, place it into the arrangement.

6 Now turn to the veronica and astilbe. Both are pointed flowers and suit the clover shape of this arrangement beautifully. Veronica also has a naturally curved shape which softens the arrangement, but unfortunately is not very efficient at retaining moisture, so it is best to remove its leaves before inserting into the display. I use ivory astilbe to contrast with the shades of purple in the arrangement, but be careful to check the balance of colour, so that nothing jars the eye. Place them at angles

into the arrangement, allowing each plenty of space. Once completed, take a look at every side of your display to check the overall balance, including the sides which should look as full as the rest of the arrangement, and not reveal any unsightly gaps. View your work from a distance and make any final adjustments you feel necessary.

FURTHER IDEAS

This design does not require many flowers, yet has plenty of movement and looks very elegant indeed.

To create the crescent base for this arrangement, shape some chicken wire and cover the base with asparagus fern. Mount a wet foam brick into the base container and affix the wire to the base. Take some virburnum, some sticks and the lily stems and insert near to the centre of the arrangement. Cut the flower heads of the lilies towards the leading edges of the crescent. Insert into glass flower/orchid tubes filled with water and fix into the wire mesh. Use the stems of asparagus fern to hide all wire and fixings. Finally, use some bun moss to hide the floral foam base.

Flowers and Greenery

- ❦ (1) Leatherleaf
- ❦ (2) Rose (Jaguar)
- ❦ (3) Spray carnation
- ❦ (4) Freesia
- ❦ (5) Sunflower
- ❦ (6) Hypericum
- ❦ (7) Italian ruscus

Materials and Equipment

- ❦ Decorative vase
- ❦ Floral foam brick
- ❦ Floral tape
- ❦ Scissors or sharp knife

ASYMMETRICAL TRIANGLE

This design is the most three-dimensional of all the arrangements in the book. I use a painted terracotta vase to show it off to its best advantage, but you can use any tall, decorative vase.

METHOD

1 Wet a foam brick, cut it to size to fit your vessel and secure it with some floral tape. Once in place, you should be able to see approximately 7cm (2¾in) of foam above its rim to accommodate some of the downwardly angled stems. Following the photo and the diagram (right), begin to work the main arteries of the arrangement. Take a

stem of Italian ruscus and cut it to a length 1½ times the height of your vase, allowing for the size and shape of the flowers and location of the arrangement. Angling it slightly backwards, insert it at 1. Once you have decided upon the length of the first stem, cut a second stem to one-third of the first and insert it at 2. Cut a further stem to two-thirds of the first and insert it at 3, the front right-hand corner of the foam brick, pitching it forwards at an angle of 45° and downwards at approximately 30°. Cut the final stem one-quarter to one-fifth of the length of the first stem and insert it at 4, the opposite left-hand corner of the foam brick. As you work, ensure that you maintain the correct angles. This is critical to the overall shape of the arrangement.

2 Now turn to the Italian ruscus and leatherleaf for the greening. Following the photo and accompanying diagram, take some of the ruscus and, angling it slightly backwards and maintaining a good bit of height, insert it at 1. Take a couple of further stems and, angling them slightly downwards, insert

them into the foam at 2 and 4 so that they tumble gently over the rim of the vase. Insert a further stem, angling it downwards on the right-hand side from the rim of the vase at 3. You should now have an almost straight line of ruscus running from 1 to 3.

3 Continue to fill in with greenery until you have a nice, full triangular shape. Insert some leatherleaf at the back of the arrangement, behind 1, to give it solidity and to disguise the back of the foam. Following the diagram, angle these slightly to follow the shape of the line from 1 to 4 to 3. This creates an

overall diamond shape at the right-hand and rear side of the arrangement, something like the leading edge of a pyramid.

4 Now turn to the hypericum and create a diagonal band of colour, working from the top left to the bottom right of the arrangement. Hypericum is a very popular garden flower and is very easy to cultivate. It produces pretty yellow flowers in summer and red berries in autumn and winter which add a seasonal touch to the

arrangement. Its leaves are also very useful and can be used as part of the greenery to make outlines or to disguise the foam base. Unfortunately the blooms are not long lasting, so, when in flower, this plant is not really suitable for use in the arrangement. Enjoy the blooms in the garden instead.

5 Next work spray carnations into the same diagonal band of colour. At this stage they will appear to be quite prominent, but will be muted by other flowers as you progress. First of all, place the flowers in bud at different heights, working in a zigzag formation along the outline from 1 to 3. Add additional buds

and blooms of a paler shade to soften the outline and darker flowers in bloom with short stems to fill in the centre. Do not forget to add some flowers behind this outline as well, and leave some stems to finish the arrangement.

6 Take the freesias and create a further diagonal band of colour. You only need add a few of these delicate flowers. Use flowers in bud with long stems to create movement within the arrangement.

7 The rose is one of the main flowers in the arrangement. Create a final band of colour, working from the top right to the bottom left of your display. This rose

is a stunning vivid red, so be aware of maintaining a good balance of colour within the arrangement. The colours in this arrangement are very striking, but you do not want any one colour to overpower the rest, and, as always, work to the principle that it is better to use too few blooms rather than too many. Following the photo as a guideline, insert one rose behind the 1–3 outline to emphasize the three-dimensional quality of this arrangement.

8 Now add the sunflowers, the second of the main flowers. Sunflower stems are very thick and fibrous, so pare them down before inserting them into the foam. Be decisive about the position of your stems to avoid creating unsightly holes in the foam. To ensure an even balance to the display, create a band of colour with the stems, working them in a zigzag formation and facing the flowers outwards along the 'outlines in the air'. To disguise the stems of the flowers at the corners of the foam, place the sunflowers with short stems from above in a downward angle. The large faces of these sunflowers will hide the corner flower stems without damaging the edge of the foam. Take a final look at the arrangement to ensure there is enough space and movement around the flowers.

FURTHER IDEAS

If you wish to do something different with your glass vase, try filling it with a selection of dried beans. Take a glass vase and hold it at an angle. Pour in some dried beans. Holding the vase at an opposite angle, pour in a second layer of different beans, gradually correcting it until the beans form another layer. Continue this technique until the jar is full. Then add the plastic dish to the centre of the top layer disguising it with flat moss but still allowing access to the foam brick in the dish. Then prepare your flower arrangement as before.

PART FOUR

Working with Curves

Flowers and Greenery

- (1) Mini gerbera
- (2) Liatris
- (3) Spray roses (Joy)
- (4) Aster
- (5) Freesia
- (6) Leatherleaf
- (7) Italian ruscus

Materials and Equipment

- Decorative shallow dish
- Plastic dish
- Floral foam brick
- Floral tape
- Frog
- Sharp knife or scissors

CRESCENT

The shape of this arrangement emulates the beautiful curve of the crescent moon. The container forms an integral part of the display, so select a container with its own intrinsic appeal, perhaps something ornate.

METHOD

1 Select a shallow, decorative dish. For this project I use an ornate, brass one. Insert a plastic dish to hold your arrangement and to avoid staining or damaging your display surface. Mount a wet floral foam brick to the dish using a frog and floral tape. Following the photo and diagram (below), begin to build the basic structure of the arrangement. Take some Italian ruscus and insert the first four stems as shown, from 1 to 4. Cut the stems at 1 and 2 to an appropriate length for the location of your arrangement or the volume of flowers you wish to use. Cut the second stem slightly shorter than the first. Cut a further two stems to one-third of the first stem. Cut a final stem to a similar length to the third

stem and insert at 5. This will create a beautiful curve from 1 through to 2 and 5. The angle at which you insert the stems at 1 and 2 should differ depending on the natural curves of the flowers you use.

For example, with lilies it is difficult to create a beautiful curve if the angle between the stems is too wide.

Depending upon the location of your arrangement, you can vary the combination of lengths of your stems. Stems 1 and 2 can be either a) the same length and inserted at the same angle, or b) the same length inserted at a different angle, or c) a different length inserted at the same angle, or finally, d) a different length inserted at a different angle. This arrangement can be created as a table centre by making both stems 3 and 4

angle downwards or as an arrangement for a hall table by inserting stem 3 vertically at the back and angling stem 4 downward at the front.

2 Now turn to the greening. Take some Italian ruscus and leatherleaf to fill out the frame of the arrangement. As you work, turn your arrangement around and check that it is balanced. It is also easier to insert greenery this way. Prepare

four stems of one-half the length of stems 1 and 2 and insert them at each side of these stems respectively. Your aim is to create an almond or rugby ball shape, as shown in the photo and diagram.

3 Now, taking the liatris, create a diagonal band of colour, working from the top right to the bottom left of the arrangement. Following the photo as a guide, place the flowers on all sides of the foam, allowing room for the greenery to stand out from behind the carefully positioned blooms, to give a sense of space and movement to the arrangement. Liatris is an excellent flower for this

display because the crescent arrangement

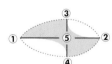

relies upon a very softly curved shape and liatris often has a thin stem which can be easily manipulated into curves. To achieve this, twist the stem between the thumb and forefinger of both hands and gently twist/stretch the skin of the stem, bending at the same time.

4 Take the spray roses and create an opposite diagonal band of colour. Cut the stems to maximum length. Use the flowers in bud with longer stems to form the outer outline and the flowers in bloom with shorter stems to fill in the centre of the arrangement. Work the flowers in a zigzag formation. Alter the height of each flower, especially those placed in the centre. As with the liatris, place some stems on the sides of the foam so that the outline of the arrangement is emphasized.

5 Now turn to the mini gerbera, one of the main flowers in the arrangement. As before, work the flowers into the arrangement in a zigzag formation. Once completed, turn the arrangement around to check the balance and movement within the display. Mini gerbera is a recent introduction to Europe and is gaining both in variety and in

popularity. Like other varieties of gerbera, it needs constant watering, but enjoys a long lifespan.

6 Use freesia here to provide an accent colour. It is really quite difficult to create an outline from 1 through 5 to 2, so use freesia buds to create more movement in the arrangement.

7 To finish the display, insert the asters. Small, delicate flowers like asters are very useful for correcting the outline and for filling any gaps. Use them sparingly to create a light, spacious effect. Before you place them into the

arrangement, cut each of the stems at the knuckle and remove the lower leaves to allow them to absorb water efficiently. Once you have completed this, look at your arrangement from the top and from the side to ensure that you have a slim cresent shape and that 5 does not hang over the outline formed by 1, 5 and 2.

FURTHER IDEAS

To create this unusual arrangement, first make a horn shape with wire netting. Take a large quantity of laurel leaves and polish them to a high shine. Using a glue gun and double-sided adhesive tape, fix the leaves to the wire shape. To do this, start from the open end, or mouth, of the shape and overlap the leaves in a 'fish scales' pattern. Place the dish holding the foam base in the open end of the cone and then arrange the flowers. You can use a foam cylinder covered in moss or laurel leaves to support the upturned end of the cone. I recommend that you use the following to create real impact: mini gerbera, rudbeckia, protea and viburnum.

Flowers and greenery

* (1) Rose (Aalsmeer Gold)

* (2) Leucadendron

* (3) Veronica

* (4) Mimosa

* (5) Leatherleaf

* (6) Spiraea

Materials and equipment

* Tall vase, display pedestal or candlestick with a cup attachment

* Plastic dish

* Floral foam brick

* Floral tape

* Frog

* Sharp knife or scissors

S SHAPE

This arrangement emulates the shape of the letter S. Although this slim version is my own design, the S shape is a classic style with beautiful flowing curves from top to bottom.

METHOD

1 For this arrangement you will require a tall vase or display pedestal/candlestick which has a cup attachment. Insert one-third of a wet foam brick in a dish and secure it using a frog, floral fix and tape. Once in place, you should be able to see approximately 3–4cm (1½in) of foam above its rim. Following the photo and diagram (see left), create the main arteries of the arrangement. Take a stem of spiraea and, angling it slightly backwards, insert it into 1. Then insert further spiraea stems into 2, 3 and 4. Cut the stem to be inserted at 2 to the same height as the vase. It should not project too far forward, so insert it at quite a low angle and tilting upwards. Cut another stem a little longer than the height of the vase

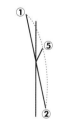

and insert at 1. Please note that the wider the line between 1 and 2, the more space there is for flowers. Cut two further stems at one-quarter to one-third of the size of the stem to be inserted at 1 and, tilting the stem slightly upwards, insert one at 3 and angling it slightly downwards, the other at 4. Cut another stem to one-third to one-quarter of the length of stem 1 and insert it at 5 making sure it is vertical.

2 Now turn to the greening for the outline. Remove any unnecessary leaves and flowers from the stems before inserting them into the arrangement. Following the photo and the accompanying diagram, begin to add the greenery. To create the S shape, add more volume to the left of

the outline between 1 and 3 and more volume to the right between 2 and 4, ensuring that each forms a nice, slim curve. Add spiraea to create the spine of the arrangement.

3 Now use the mimosa to form the outlines. Mimosa flowers are pale yellow when in bud and bright golden yellow when in bloom, so cut the stems to maximum length while you consider the balance between the two in the arrangement. If you have some mimosa flowers which are not yet in bloom and you would like them to be, you can force them to do so by placing the stems into a bucket of warm water which you should then cover with a plastic bag. This acts in much the same way as a greenhouse. Leave them covered for a day or two and you will see the buds begin to open. Do

not keep them covered for too long, however, because too much humidity causes the flowers to turn brown.

4 Following the photo and the accompanying diagram (below), create a diagonal band of colour with the veronica. Cut the stems to different lengths and insert them at varying angles to create movement in the bottom half of the arrangement. Work them in from the top left to the bottom right of the arrangement, from 1 to 5 to 2. Although the stems are quite straight, make the most of the natural curves of the flower heads to emphasize the S shape of the outline. Do not place long stems into the top right or bottom left of the arrangement or the S shape will distort into an oval. Instead, use just enough

shorter stems to cover the rim of the dish. Once this has been completed, disguise the stems with greenery and flowers.

5 Now turn to the Aalsmeer Gold roses. Insert them into the arrangement, forming an S shape curve as you work. Alter the angle of each flower, turning the heads in slightly different directions along the 'outlines in the air' to give movement and balance to the arrangement. Disguise the bottom of any visible longer stems by placing short-stemmed roses into the arrangement. Place them from the top in order to disguise the stems more effectively from view.

6 Leucadendron, which is also commonly known as Red Sunset, originates from South Africa and provides an exotic contrast to the rose. The

leucadendron is a very chic flower and its striking colour works very well with the yellow rose in this arrangement. They are extremely complementary flowers and I like to work them together where I can. The leucadendron also has the advantage of being extremely long lasting. This flower does, however, have a thick stem, so remove the leaves from the lower stem and pare it down using a sharp knife in order to avoid making unnecessarily large holes in the floral foam base and to ensure that, once placed, the stems stay firmly in position.

7 Finally, to add some rhythm to your display, add blooms of spiraea throughout the arrangement.

8 Viewing the arrangement from all sides, including the side view, check that the S shape looks balanced and that the floral foam base is well disguised with greenery. Make any adjustments required to achieve this. Your arrangement should now be complete.

FURTHER IDEAS

If you wish, you can recreate this design horizontally as a feature for a table setting which beautifully softens the lines of the table. This display makes use of pussy willow, lysimachia, Jacaranda rose, freesia and asparagus fern. Additionally, you can add candles to the centre. Use the same materials to create matching napkin rings. To bend the willow for the napkin rings without breaking it, use both your thumbs to twist the stem as you gently bend it into shape.

Flowers and Greenery

- (1) Leatherleaf
- (2) Rose (Gerdo)
- (3) Lily (Vivaldi)
- (4) Antirrhinum
- (5) Spray carnations
- (6) Pittosporum
- (7) Italian ruscus

Materials and Equipment

- Oval-shaped plastic dish
- Floral foam brick
- Frog and floral fix
- Floral tape
- Sharp knife or scissors

L SHAPE

This design is formed in the shape of the letter L. It beautifully complements items such as framed mirrors, and is delightful set against a deep mantel shelf.

METHOD

1 Take an oval display dish, wet half a floral foam brick and secure it to the dish using a frog, floral fix and tape. Take some Italian ruscus and

insert the stems into 1, 2, 3 and 4, the main arteries of the arrangement. The length of your first stem will depend upon the size of your location. Cut the first stem to an appropriate length to fit, or perhaps to line up with either a mirror or picture frame. For this arrangement, I cut it to 45cm (18in) in length. Cut a second stem to two-thirds of the length of the first and insert it at 2. Cut two further stems to one-third of the first. Following the photo and accompanying diagram (above), insert these stems into position.

2 Now turn to the greening. Take a stem of Italian ruscus and, angling it slightly backwards, insert it into the arrangement. Angle all remaining stems slightly downwards from the rim of the dish. As you work, pay attention to the outlines, particularly for the side view, as

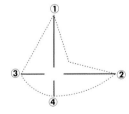

shown in the diagram. The frame formed by 1, 2 and 3 is a triangular shape. 1 to 2 forms the letter L and 2, 4 and 3 forms a frontal bow shape. Angle the stem at 4 slightly downwards. To disguise the foam and create the backing, take some leatherleaf and insert it into the arrangement. Keep the backing leaves short-stemmed at the corner of the L- angle to emphasize its shape.

3 For colour contrast and to add relief to the display, add the variegated pittosporum judiciously to the arrangement. If you do not have pittosporum, you can use similar variegated leaves from your garden.

Take a look at the outline between 1 and 4 to check that your arrangement is upright and not bending forwards. The wider the space between 1 and 4, the more space there is to add flowers. By giving the flowers plenty of space, you can use many of them and still create movement in the arrangement.

4 Next, turn to the spray carnations, one of the main flowers. Create a band of colour with the stems by cutting them to maximum length and begin to place them into the the arrangement from the top. Remember to keep the volume of the spray carnations equal on the vertical and horizontal line. These flowers are available all year round in Europe, with the exception of this peach variety, which is not available in winter. It grows from spring to autumn and is popular for wedding arrangements.

5 Antirrhinum is another main flowerin the arrangement. Create a diagonal band of colour, working from the top left to the bottom right of the arrangement. Cut them only at the very

bottom of the stem and place them at a vertical angle within

the arrangement, positioning them to make the most of their height. Antirrhinums also grow towards the light, so in order to keep the beautiful shape of the arrangement, rotate the stems occasionally.

6 Use the lilies to create an opposite diagonal band of colour, working from right to left. Place one lily high up to create a cascading line of lilies in the arrangement. Place another at the right angle of the L shape to emphasize its shape. This also creates depth in the arrangement. Place a further lily just in front of the one at the angle for rhythm. As you work, remember to handle the lilies

carefully to avoid spoiling them.

7 Finally, place the roses. These provide a contrast of size and texture to the lilies and the antirrhinums, and also add brightness to the whole arrangement. Work the roses in a zigzag formation in between the other main flowers, repeatedly standing at a distance to check the volume and balance of flowers on the vertical and horizontal axes, and that they are within the outline formed by 1 and 4. Make any

adjustments necessary to achieve a balanced display. Do not forget to add flowers to the sides and back of the arrangement so that it can be viewed from all sides.

This variation on the L shape floral design is very dramatic thanks to the beautiful arum lily, the key flower in the arrangement. The display would be particularly effective for the corner of a grand hallway or suit a more formal occasion. The arrangement can be completed in much the same way as before, except you will requre a display pedestal. Other flowers and foliage which would work well here are variegated ivy to train around the pedestal, and curly willow to add further drama. The calla, or arum, lily has a soft stem and can therefore be difficult to insert into the foam. Inserting a cocktail stick or piece of natural straw about 10cm (4in) long into the end of the stem, or taping it to the outside, will give the lily extra support. Once complete, position the arrangement alongside a mirror or window for a stunning display.

Flowers and Greenery

- ❧ (1) Leatherleaf
- ❧ (2) Rose (Cocktail)
- ❧ (3) Myrtle
- ❧ (4) Pepper
- ❧ (5) Calla lily
- ❧ (6) Crocosmia
- ❧ (7) Mimosa
- ❧ (8) Italian ruscus

Materials and Equipment

- ❧ Plastic dish
- ❧ Floral foam brick
- ❧ Floral tape
- ❧ Sharp knife or scissors

L SHAPE TABLE CENTRE

This arrangement is perfect for decorating the corner of a rectangular table – perhaps for a smart buffet party or wedding reception.

METHOD

1 All you require to display this arrangement is a plastic dish. Wet one-third of a floral foam brick and secure it with floral tape. Create the main arteries of the arrangement with Italian ruscus. Cut the first stem to a quarter of the length of the table upon which the arrangement will feature. Following the photo and the accompanying diagram, insert the stem at 1. Cut a second stem to two-thirds of the length of the first stem and insert it at 2. The angle between stems 1 and 2 should be slightly wider than 90° to emphasize the L shape. Cut two further stems to one-third of the length of stem 1 to be inserted at 3 and 4. The final stem, to be inserted at 5, can be any length you like, in line with the length of the other flowers in your arrangement. I have cut it to one-third of the length of the first stem.

2 Take stems of Italian ruscus, leatherleaf and myrtle and insert them around the rim of the dish, angling them downwards towards the table. This not only gives the flowers in your arrangement a sense of space and movement, but disguises the dish. First work the outline of the arrangement with Italian ruscus and then add stems of leatherleaf and myrtle for emphasis.

3 Create a diagonal band of colour with the mimosa, working from the top left to the bottom right of the arrangement. Insert the pale yellow mimosa buds with longer stems to create the outline and use the flowers in bloom

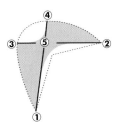

with shorter stems to fill the centre. As you work, check the balance of colour and volume of flowers in your arrangement. Place stems at the bottom of the arrangement in the side of the foam so that they are parallel to the surface of the table. Leave some stems to finish off the display later on.

4 Now turn to the peppers. In Europe, peppers and paprikas are often used for Christmas arrangements. They are available in many colours: green, red, orange, yellow and creamy white, and in different shapes, both pointed or round. They can also be used as dry flowers for floral arrangements. The variety that I use for this arrangement appears in the florist shops in winter and

I like to select those that are just turning red. Pepper stems are rather thick, so pare them down a bit using a sharp knife before placing them into the foam. Now create an opposite diagonal band of colour to the mimosa.

5 Calla, or arum lily, is one of the main flowers in the arrangement. Following the photo, place the stems. The stems are naturally curved, so it is important to select the right position to

display them to their best advantage. If you find the stems are too soft and malleable, support them from underneath with thin stems of mimosa or Italian ruscus. Always ensure that you use fresh stems which will absorb water more efficiently.

6 This rusty yellow cocktail rose is another main flower in the arrangement. In Britain, rusty yellow is called golden yellow, which is why it is

popular to send fifty yellow roses to those celebrating a golden anniversary. Create an outline with the longer stems of flowers in bud and place the flowers in bloom with shorter stems in the centre. Cut each flower to a slightly different height and alter their angles to create a sense of movement.

7 Next, turn to the deep orange crocosmia which provides excellent contrast to the other colours in the arrangement. Place flowers and leaves downwards to cover the dish beneath. As you work, check the shape of the arrangement from above and from every other side, too, to ensure that you have a well balanced display.

8 Finally, fill any gaps with mimosa and greenery which will also emphasize the outlines. Place flowers at the back to add depth and weight and give the correct proportions. Think of the arrangement as a mountain, whereby the top, at 5, is the peak, and the remaining flowers cascade down at different heights

to create movement. Check the L shape in the arrangement by positioning it at the corner of your table. Although the angle between 1 and 2 is more obtuse than a conventional L shape, it will appear perfectly aligned due to the volume of flowers.

FURTHER IDEAS

A striking alternative to the floral display is the vegetable arrangement shown above. Using vegetables and herbs from the garden and arranging them in an L shape, this arrangement is particularly effective for decorating an unusual summer lunch or supper table – or perhaps a harvest festival table.

Flowers and Greenery

- ❦ (1) Asparagus fern
- ❦ (2) Astilbe
- ❦ (3) Dendrobium
- ❦ (4) Anthurium
- ❦ (5) Leatherleaf
- ❦ (6) Italian ruscus

Materials and Equipment

- ❦ Floral foam brick
- ❦ Floral tape
- ❦ Plastic dish
- ❦ Sharp knife or scissors

CRESCENT TABLE CENTRE

This arrangement is quite different from the L shape table centre, and is suitable for a round table. It has a special significance for me because I was commissioned to design it for a reception for Princess Anne, the Princess Royal.

METHOD

1 Take a plastic dish, wet one-third of a foam brick and secure to the dish using floral tape. Take the first stem of leatherleaf and cut it to fit into the curve of the round table to a maximum length of one third of the perimeter. Following the photo and accompanying diagram, above, insert the stem at 1. Cut another stem to two-thirds of the length of the first and insert it at 2. Cut three further stems of the same length, one-third of the length of the first stem and insert them at 3, 4 and 5. Stem 5 should be inserted vertically into the top centre of the foam.

2 Using Italian ruscus and asparagus fern, turn to the greening. Insert a long stem of Italian ruscus directly behind the stem inserted at 1. Cut several short stems and then form the outline created by 1, 4 and 2 on the diagram. It is a very slim outline, intended only to disguise the edge of the dish. As demonstrated in the photo, right, the outline formed by 1, 3

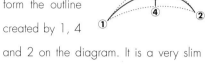

and 2 should form a parallel curve to that of 1, 4 and 2. Insert some asparagus fern to create movement. Once this is completed, disguise the foam with additional greenery.

3 Now turn to the dendrobium. Cut four stems to maximum length. You require only three different flowers for this arrangement and do not, therefore, need to create the bands of colour required for previous arrangements. The natural beauty of each individual flower is more

important here. Following the outlines shown in the photo, above, and diagram, below left, place dendrobium throughout the arrangement along the outlines. Use flowers in bud with longer stems to form the outlines and flowers in bloom with shorter stems to fill the centre.

4 Next, arrange the astilbe in a diagonal band. Astilbe varies in size according to the season. If your astilbe is in flower, place the fluffy, pointed top half into the arrangement to create movement and use the leafy

continued on page 78

FURTHER IDEAS

You can adapt the crescent table centre arrangement in other ways. Fit a half ring of foam to a dish or bowl, preferably one with a lip, dress it with flowers and greenery and fill its centre with water, matching coloured glass pebbles and floating candles. For this arrangement I use red roses. If you do so and they begin to wilt, wrap them tightly in newspaper, with their heads together, allowing 10cm (4in) of stem to protrude at the base. Dip them in 4cm (1¼in) of boiling hot water for approximately 2 minutes then plunge into cold water and soak for 2 hours. This will give them a new lease of life.

continued from page 76

bottom half to fill any gaps. To emphasize contrast, keep their stems long. Astilbe does not absorb water easily, so cut it above the knuckle to encourage water absorption. It is also best to remove as many of its leaves as you can which you can use as greenery elsewhere in the arrangement.

5 Anthurium is the main flower in the arrangement. It is a flat-shaped flower, varies in size and colour and makes a dramatic impact. Following the photo, above, work it in a zigzag formation. As you work, observe the shape of each flower and alter its height to maintain the crescent shape of the arrangement and its angle to create movement. When you buy the flowers, they are usually well packed. Remove the packing material as soon as you can to guard against high humidity which tends to turn the flowers brown. In addition,

order your flowers for immediate use as anthuriums do not last well.

6 Finally, use asparagus fern to create a sense of movement. If there are any gaps between flowers, place a few further stems grouped together. You can use some leatherleaf for the same purpose. Take a look at your completed arrangement from all sides, including from above and behind, to check that the dish is disguised and that the flowers are evenly distributed throughout the arrangement. Remember to place one brightly coloured flower to the rear face of the arrangement to make a bold gesture.

Flowers and Greenery

- ❧ (1) Bouvardia
- ❧ (2) Polygonum
- ❧ (3) Spray carnations
- ❧ (4) Rose (Sonia)
- ❧ (5) September
- ❧ (6) Leatherleaf
- ❧ (7) Calistemon

Materials and Equipment

- ❧ Urn style vase
- ❧ Floral foam brick
- ❧ Floral tape
- ❧ Sharp knife or scissors

HOGARTH

This style is very similar to the S shape arrangement and is named after the eighteenth-century English artist William Hogarth who famously theorized that the S-shaped curve was the ultimate 'line of beauty'.

METHOD

1 Wet one-third of a floral foam brick and secure it to the urn style vase with floral tape. Try to use a vase moulded to a classical style rather than a modern one to emphasize the beautiful shape of this design. Many of the flowers will be placed from below at an upward angle, so ensure that the foam base is mounted about 6cm (2⅓in) higher than the rim of the dish. Now create the main arteries of the arrangement with the calistemon. Cut the first stem to one and a half times the height of the vase and insert it into the left-hand side of the foam, angling it upwards and slightly inwards. Following the references closely (see the photos, above, and the diagram, right), cut a second stem slightly shorter than the first and, bending it gently with your fingers to form a curve in the stem, place it into the right-hand side of the foam at 2. The head of the stem should reach across the front of the vase at an angle. Cut a

further three stems to the same length, one-third of the length of the first stem, and insert at 3, 4 and 5. Turn the vase 90°, so that its handle faces you directly. The stem at 3 should stand vertically in the centre of the right-hand side of the foam, and curve upwards. The stem at 4 should be slightly shorter than the stem at 3 and positioned in the left-hand side of the foam and angled downwards and backwards towards the stem inserted at 2. You now have a basic S shape.

2 Now turn to the greening. Following the photo, above, and diagram, below, arrange the top half of the Hogarth display in the approximate shape of a half-oval by inserting two stems, one on either side of the stem at 1. Arrange the bottom half of the arrangement

similarly, into a twisted half-oval, angled out from one side of the foam. Insert leatherleaf and polygonum to complete the frame and to disguise the foam base, altering the height of each stem and its position, to maintain the shape.

3 Keep the handle of the urn facing you directly. It is easier to continue building the oval shape for the top half of the arrangement from this position. Begin to place

spray carnations in a diagonal band, working from the top right to the bottom left of the arrangement. Following the photo and the accompanying diagram, above, place flowers in bud with longer stems to create an outline and flowers in bloom with shorter stems to fill the centre.

4 Next, turn to the roses. Place them in another diagonal band of colour,

working from the top left to the bottom right of the arrangement. Near the rim of the vase, place roses into the side of the foam which allows more space for inserting other flowers later. By varying the angle at which you place the stems, you will create less damage to the surface of the foam base. As you work, ensure that you maintain an equal volume of flowers for both halves of the arrangement.

5 Turn your urn so that it is facing frontwards once more. At this stage, you will have some gaps in your flowers at the front of the arrangement. Fill in the outlines at the front, turning the vase from side to front occasionally to ensure that you achieve the twisted shape of the arrangement. It is important to check the overall balance as this

81

arrangement should be enjoyed from many vantage points.

6 Bouvardia is one of the main flowers in the arrangement. It is a delicate flower, available in white, pink, red, and in single and double blooms. Keep the stems cut as short as possible to absorb the water more efficiently. To give the flowers a good start, water them thoroughly before placing them into the arrangement. You can also prolong the life of the flower by investing in cut flower food which is widely available. Work them in a zigzag formation, altering the height of each to create a sense of movement.

7 Finally, place the September, which is a kind of aster. These are used here to emphasize the outlines as well as to create rhythm in the arrangement as a

whole. In this arrangement, I have used two medium-sized flowers rather than a larger one. This is to emphasize a sense of harmony and bring softly curved lines

to the arrangement, rather than the individual character of the flowers themselves. Whichever flowers you use, keep this sense of harmony and softness in mind. Take some leatherleaf and place into the back of the arrangement to disguise the rear face of the foam. View the arrangement from all sides to ensure that the top and the bottom halves have equal volume of flowers.

8 Your arrangement is now complete. As you can see in the photo, the arrangement is formed by two outlines, one beautifully curved between 1 and 5 and a further twisted one between 5 and 2. If you are selecting your own flowers for this arrangement, try to choose ones which have a natural curve which will emphasize the S shape of the arrangement.

FURTHER IDEAS

You can create a similar arrangement using different flowers altogether, for example willow, delphinum, Tineke rose, gerbera, senecio cineraria leaves and cotoneaster leaves. Adapt the shape to one which is more slimline by tapering the curve of the lazy S shape a little longer at the top than the bottom. Delphiniums are wonderful for this arrangement. They have a hollow stem which can be difficult to insert into the foam base, so insert a cocktail stick or piece of natural straw about 10cm (4in) into the base of the stem to give it support. Flowers which have hollow stems are often very thirsty, so make sure that you water the final arrangement frequently so that it does not dry out.

PART FIVE

Geometric
Arrangements

Flowers and Greenery

- ❦ (1) Leatherleaf
- ❦ (2) Aster
- ❦ (3) Lily (Apeldoorn, or other variety of orange lily)
- ❦ (4) Amaranthus
- ❦ (5) Fennel
- ❦ (6) Liatris
- ❦ (7) Italian ruscus

Materials and Equipment

- ❦ Trough-style plastic dish
- ❦ Floral foam brick
- ❦ Floral tape
- ❦ Frog and floral fix
- ❦ Sharp knife or scissors

RECTANGLE

The rectangle arrangement is possibly the most natural of all the arrangements in the book. It almost looks as though a little bit of the garden has simply been brought into the house!

METHOD

1 Take a rectangular plastic dish, wet a whole floral foam brick, and secure it in the dish using a frog. floral fix and tape. Following the photo, above, and the diagram, right, take some Italian ruscus and create the main arteries of the arrangement, from 1 to 4. Cut the first stem to a length of 45cm (18in) and insert it at 1. Cut a second stem to around one-half or two-thirds of the first stem and insert it at 2. Cut a further stem to a length midway between the first and second stems and insert it at 3. These stems should all be inserted at the back of the foam brick to leave space for the rest of the flowers and greenery. Cut a final stem one-third to one-quarter of

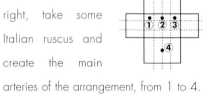

the length of the first stem and place at 4.

2 Now turn to the greening. Take some Italian ruscus and leatherleaf and, working from the edge of the dish rather than the foam, form a vertical, rectangular frame of leaves. If you work within the edge of the foam only, the frame of the arrangement will not be wide enough. Ensure that the stems at the back of the arrangement, at 1, 2 and 3, angle slightly backwards and that the stem at 4 angles slightly downwards. This will provide a little more room for the flowers. Angle the stems at the front of

the arrangement forwards to cover the edge of the dish. Following the photo and accompanying diagram, when working either end of the foam brick,

angle the stems upwards to maintain a rectangular frame at the back. Cut the leatherleaf shorter than the Italian ruscus and insert both into the back of the arrangement to add to the frame and to disguise the foam and the dish.

3 On the top face of the foam, those flowers which are in the centre and those nearer the edges should all be placed at a vertical angle. If in doubt, consult the main photograph of the arrangement. On the rear face of the foam, flowers should be angled backwards, and on the front of the foam those nearest to the rim of the dish should be angled downwards. The angles at which you place each individual flower should be slightly different, thus allowing plenty of space around each bloom. Complete the backing of the arrangement to make a wall for the display.

4 Take the liatris and create a diagonal band of colour, working from the top left to the bottom right of the arrangement. Cut the stem of the liatris to maximum length so that it stands higher in the arrangement than the outline of the greening and insert the first stem 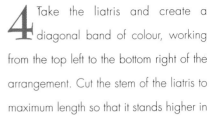 of liatris at 1. Increasingly shorten the stems of liatris to graduate downwards in height and across the arrangement, from top left to bottom front right (see the photo, right and diagram, above). Make certain that they are nice, straight stems.

5 Next turn to the lilies. Create a diagonal band of colour, working from the top right to bottom left. Place flowers in bud with longer stems into the arrangement to form the outline and flowers in bloom with shorter stems to fill the centre. As you position each individual lily, rotate it to observe which is the perfect angle to make the most impact for the arrangement as a whole. If you happen to have some well-formed lily leaves, put them to one side to use as greenery. Check the balance of lilies in the display and, if necessary, add a short-stemmed lily at the back of the arrangement for dramatic impact.

6 Amaranthus is a pointed flower and, when used in contrast with a round-headed flower like the lily, lends an arrangement a wonderful cottage garden feel. Before you place the stems, remove

most of the leaves so that the stems can absorb water more efficiently and to give the flowers more space. Create a diagonal band, working from the top right to bottom left of the arrangement. Commonly known as 'Love lies bleeding', the red variety of amaranthus is a popular flower in Europe and is increasingly fashionable in flower design. It is also very easy to dry and use in dried flower arrangements.

7 Fennel is a round mass flower and contrasts beautifully with the liatris. It is also very useful for filling gaps, but should be used judiciously as it can make the arrangement flat and boring. If you do not have fennel, other good alternatives are lace flower and dill. Place the fennel in the same diagonal band as the liatris. For the front half of the arrangement, cut the short stems and place them straight into the top of the foam. If you place them at an angle, the whole arrangement will lose its movement.

8 Finally, arrange the asters into the arrangement. It is used here to emphasize the outline as well as to disguise the stems of the other flowers. Cut some of the stems a little shorter to disguise the foam, too. Before you begin, remove any unnecessary leaves. As you work, view the arrangement from a distance as well as close up, paying attention to the balance of colour and movement. As you can see in the photo,

FURTHER IDEAS

Derived from a style of flower arranging developed in the 1960s known as 'pot-et-fleur', this arrangement is created with both flower stems and greenery, cut flowers and house plants. For ease and speed, fill the trough container with mainly bedding plants (still in their individual pots) and plant directly into the foam, adding other cut flowers, like forsythia, mimosa, tulips, etc. to suit the arrangement. For a more impressive display, make up multiple troughs and group them together, perhaps, as shown opposite, to create a springtime display for a church Easter celebration.

you should allow plenty of space around the flower heads which emulates the way these flowers grow in the garden.

9 Your arrangement is now complete. It looks very striking on a window ledge in any room of the house or, alternatively, used to decorate the speaker's table at a conference or other special event. Several of these arrangements placed together can be used to create a charming miniature garden in your home.

Flowers and Greenery

- ❦ (1) Leatherleaf
- ❦ (2) Rose (Europa)
- ❦ (3) Trachelium
- ❦ (4) Lily (Star Gazer)
- ❦ (5) Lisianthus
- ❦ (6) Statice
- ❦ (7) Pittosporum
- ❦ (8) Liatris
- ❦ (9) Italian ruscus

Materials and Equipment

- ❦ Deep crystal display dish
- ❦ Floral foam brick
- ❦ Floral tape
- ❦ Frog and floral fix
- ❦ Sharp knife or scissors

CONE SHAPE

In the Byzantine era, the cone shape was a very popular one for use in topiary, but has since gained favour in natural flower arrangement. It is a wonderful shape, allowing lots of movement, yet presenting a cohesive whole that is very satisfying.

METHOD

1 Take a deep crystal dish, wet two thirds of a foam and secure it to the dish using a frog, floral fix and tape. Following the photo, above, and the diagram, left, take a stem of Italian ruscus and cut it to an appropriate length to fit the location of your arrangement, or to comfortably fit your chosen dish. I have cut it to 45cm (18in). Insert it vertically into the centre of the foam at 1. Cut five further leatherleaf stems to one-third of the length of the first stem. Insert these at 2, 3, 4, 5 and 6, angling them downwards from the rim of the dish.

2 Now turn to the greening using Italian ruscus, leatherleaf and pittosporum. The flat shape of the leatherleaf provides a nice contrast to the Italian ruscus and pittosporum which create a sense of movement. Consider the stem at 1 to be the centre of the arrangement and work the leaves around

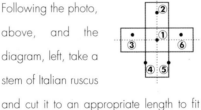

this stem to form a circular five-pronged star shape when viewed from above. Gradually shorten the stems of greenery as you approach the rim of the circle. In the accompanying photo and diagram, you can see the frame of a cone shape from 1 to 2 to 6. As you insert the stems for 2 to 6, angle them downwards to disguise the foam base. Insert those stems in the centre of the arrangement vertically and angle those nearer the edges slightly outwards. Insert those stems in the side of the foam horizontally, and angle those nearest to the rim of the dish downwards.

3 Taking stems of liatris and cutting them to maximum length, create a diagonal band of colouring in the arrangement. Their heads should rise above those of the Italian ruscus. Take a look at the

arrangement from all sides to check the balance of elements. I find it helpful to secure a turntable to either the surface of a table or on the floor in order to view the arrangement more easily.

4 Take stems of statice and cut them to maximum length. Now create a second diagonal band of colour, working from the front of the arrangement, over the top, to the back. Statice is smaller in size and paler in colour than liatris, so pay attention to the balance of colour and volume between the two in the arrangement. Statice is very useful for emphasizing outlines and for movement, so put aside some stems to finish the arrangement later.

5 Now turn to the lilies and lisianthus. These flowers are so different in character that they offer a nice contrast to one another in the arrangement – as long as you keep an eye on the balance between them. Cut the stems of both the lilies and the lisianthus to give maximum length to the arrangement. Work the lilies in bud along the outlines and insert the lilies in bloom into the bottom of the

arrangement. Once open, lisianthus is boldly coloured so, for impact, use it predominantly in the centre of the arrangement and the lilies at the bottom.

6 Trachelium is a mass flower, which means that its head is made up of tiny, round flowers massed together. It is a native of Europe, and is available in purple and white. It is not a key flower, but enhances the more prominent flowers in the arrangement. If the flowers are gathered in a large mass, remove some before you begin and put these to one side in case you wish to use them later. Cut the stems to give maximum length and insert into the arrangement.

7 To finish, insert the roses. They can be placed throughout the arrangement. As you work, check the balance of the flowers in the arrangement and its shape by turning and viewing it all round, particularly the sides. Ensure that the flower faces conform to the 'outlines in the air'. As you look at the finished arrangement, notice the way the flowers are co-ordinated into colour groups, from pale pink to violet. This technique is, perhaps obviously, known as 'colour graduation'. If you wish, vary the height of the arrangement and volume of flowers used to suit any location or occasion.

FURTHER IDEAS

For a very different cone shape effect, create an arrangement like the one shown here. Position three glass or crystal decanters together, each holding a Conneticut King lily. You can use alternative lilies for this arrangement, as long as you use a variety with the blooms at the top of the stem, rather than as offshoots from the stem itself, for example La Reve. Wire the three lily heads together just below the blooms. Take a circular foam wreath, cut it in half and rearrange to form an S shape. Position it at each side of the group of decanters. Take the ruscus leaves and, starting from one end, mould each leaf into a trumpet shape and pin to the foam base. Once you have completed three layers of leaves, pin a band of moss to the foam and continue to pin the bands of trumpet-shaped leaves. Continue with this technique until you reach the end of the curve. Ensure that you make an equal number of bands on each curve. If you wish, create a third curved wreath and insert it into the remaining space between decanters.

Flowers and Greenery

- ❦ (1) Ornithogalum (Arabicum)
- ❦ (2) Leatherleaf
- ❦ (3) Solidago
- ❦ (4) Chrysanthemum
- ❦ (5) Lysimachia
- ❦ (6) Carnations
- ❦ (7) Viburnum tinus
- ❦ (8) Pittosporum

Materials and Equipment

- ❦ Large oval-shaped display bowl
- ❦ Floral foam brick
- ❦ Floral tape
- ❦ Sharp knife or scissors

FAN SHAPE

This design is inspired by the beautiful shape of an open fan and is always a popular arrangement for its elegant curves. It is a pleasing arrangement to create because the shape allows you plenty of space to use lots of different flowers.

METHOD

1 Take a large oval-shaped bowl, wet one-third of a foam brick, and secure it to the dish using floral tape. Once in place, you should be able to see approximately 3–4cm (1½in) of foam above its rim. Following the photo, above, and diagram, right, begin to arrange the main lines with pittosporum, working from 1 to 4. Keeping in mind the location for the arrangement, cut the first stem to the appropriate length. It should be cut rather longer than normal because the main flower, the chrysanthemum, is quite large and everything should balance. I have cut the first stem here to 50cm (20in). Cut

two further stems slightly longer than two-thirds of the first stem and insert these at 2 and 3. Angle these stems to make the most of the natural curve of the pittosporum. Cut a final stem slightly longer than one-third of the first stem and insert it at 4.

2 Taking some pittosporum and leatherleaf, turn to the greening. Following the accompanying photo and diagram, below, begin to work on the fan shape of the arrangement. Insert two long stems of pittosporum on either side of the stem at 1. You will notice that you have a nice long bow-shaped line from 2 through 4 to 3 which will allow plenty of space for the flowers.

Arrange leatherleaf around the rim of the bowl to emphasize the frame you have created as well as to disguise the floral foam base.

3 Using the lysimachia, create a diagonal band of colour, working from top right to bottom left. In order to create a natural, spacious feel, angle the flowers slightly backwards at the back of the foam base. Like veronica, lysimachia has a natural curve, so take advantage of this when working the outlines. It also has a pointed character, so keep the stems nice and long to emphasize movement.

4 Now turn to the ornithogalum. This type has longer stems and larger flowers than others on the market, so do endeavour to find it. When it is in blossom, it forms a ball-like shape and is black in the centre, adding a little subtle drama to the arrangement. It is wonderful to use because it is a very long lasting flower, normally lasting up to two weeks. Working in the opposite direction to the lysimachia, place the ornithogalum in another diagonal band from top left to bottom right. Again, angle them slightly backwards on the back of the foam. Use the flowers in bud with longer stems to make an outline, and flowers in

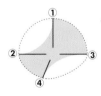

bloom with shorter stems to fill the centre of the arrangement. Ornithogalum has no leaves, so try to ensure that the stems you use are disguised with other flowers or greenery.

5 Next, arrange the chrysanthemum, the main flower in the arrangement. Here I have used a chrysanthemum with a large yellow-green flower. Try to select those with longer stems as the flower head is quite large and ideally requires some space. If you use shorter stems, the arrangement will lack movement. When placing those stems in the top of the foam, ensure that they are vertical.

7a

6 Take the carnations and work a diagonal band from the top left to bottom right of the arrangement. These work to balance with the large chrysanthemums and the small lysimachia. The three round-headed flowers, the chrysanthemum, ornithogalum and carnations, are used to decorate the centre, whereas the lysimachia enhances the outline. To ensure that the arrangement adheres to the 'colour graduation' approach, ensure that you insert the carnations within the outline. Otherwise, you risk upsetting the fan shape

7 Finally, add the solidago and viburnum tinus. The solidago is similar to solidaster and used to form an outline. The viburnum tinus is used to fill in the centre of the display. The flowers of viburnum tinus are small and pink and its berries a pretty pearl blue. You can use the viburnum with or without berries, according to the season. Place stems of both throughout the arrangement to create depth and lend a natural feel. As you work, look at the photos and the diagram to get a sense of the overall shape of the arrangement. From the side, your display should lean slightly backwards to open up space for the chrysanthemums. Finally, take some leatherleaf and angle it backwards on the reverse face of the foam for the backing, and to give depth. The backing forms a number of functions: to disguise the foam, emphasize the frame of the arrangement, and bring out the character of the flowers.

7b

7c

FURTHER IDEAS

This variation on the fan shape arrangement makes maximum use of your garden, particularly if you have fruit trees. If you create the arrangement in late spring, trim some of the branches from your fruit trees to add to it. If you can find ornamental cabbage, or you grow it yourself, you may add it to the bottom of this kind of arrangement. Other plants which go very well in the arrangement are anthurium, Casa Blanca lily, euphorbia and delphinium.

Flowers and greenery

- ❧ (1) Asparagus fern
- ❧ (2) Rose (Golden Times)
- ❧ (3) Astilbe
- ❧ (4) Limonium
- ❧ (5) Alstroemeria
- ❧ (6) Tulip (Yokohama)
- ❧ (7) Carnation
- ❧ (8) Italian ruscus

Materials and equipment

- ❧ Shallow crystal display dish
- ❧ Floral foam brick
- ❧ Floral tape
- ❧ Frog and floral fix
- ❧ Sharp knife or scissors

VERTICAL STAR SHAPE

This design is very elegant indeed, making full use of straight, vertical lines and a five-pronged star shape at the bottom. Make the most of this design and create a large arrangement to be displayed in a prominent location for real impact.

METHOD

1 Take a shallow crystal dish, wet half of a foam brick and secure it to the dish using a frog, floral fix and tape. Once in place, you should be able to see approximately 3–4cm (1½in) of foam above its rim. Following the photos, below and right, and accompanying diagram, take some Italian ruscus and asparagus fern and begin to create the main arteries of the arrangement, working from 1 to 6. Taking into consideration the location for your arrangement or the length of the stems that you have, cut the first stem

to an appropriate length. For this arrangement, I have cut it to 45cm (17½in). Insert the first stem at 1. Since it has a tendency to bend slightly, insert the Italian ruscus slightly shorter than the vertical outline and into the top face of the foam. Prepare five further stems at two-thirds of the length of the first stem. Following the diagram, insert these at 2, 3, 4, 5 and 6. They should be inserted in equal balance to maintain the five-pronged star shape. If you want to create a more open and pronounced shape, cut the stems for 2 to 6 a little longer. On the sides of the foam base, your stems should be horizontal,

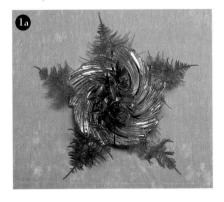

but angle those nearest to the rim of the dish downwards. As you work, take a look at the arrangement from the top. The stems in the centre should be vertical whilst those nearer the edges should be angled at 90° Indeed, you should

have a star shape formed by the asparagus ferns at the bottom and perfectly vertical stems of Italian ruscus. Now take a look at the side view of the arrangement. It should look like a backwards letter L. Pay attention to the vertical and horizontal lines and the amount of space opened up for the rest of the flowers.

2 Now turn to the astilbe. Insert the stems in a band, working from the back of the arrangement to the front, via the top. Astilbe is a pointed flower which makes it very suitable for this arrangement. It is used as the apex of the arrangement and will stand higher than the Italian ruscus stem at 1. Take another stem of astilbe, slightly shorter than the first, and place it in the centre of the arrangement. Ensure that the head of the second flower meets the stem of the first at the top. It is more important to achieve this than to place them at a perfectly vertical angle into the arrangement. In this instance, you do not need to remove the leaves from the astilbe before you arrange them.

3 Now take some limonium and cut the stems to achieve maximum length. Work a further band of colour from front to back of the arrangement. Limonium has a mass of small, soft, purple flowers on each stem. For volume, group a few stems together. Following the photo, left, place the stems along the outlines. As you work, ensure that you do not place flowers too heavily on the bottom of the arrangement, since it will become a cone shape arrangement rather than a vertical star shape.

4 Next, take some tulips and work a band of colour in the opposite direction to the band of astilbe. Cut the stems of the tulips a little shorter than the astilbe to avoid making the vertical line too heavy. For the bottom half of the arrangement, particularly near the edge of the foam, place only the tulips with very short stems. For the main lines of the arrangement, place the tulips horizontally, angling them slightly downwards. Do not form an overly acute angle, however, or the arrangement will lose its shape. Finally, ensure that you leave a distinct space in the inside corner of each of the L shapes of the star shape, placing only flower heads, rather than full stems, to fill this space.

5 Now turn to the carnations and alstroemeria. Carnation is a round-headed flower and is intended here to fill any gaps in the arrangement. Place one long stem vertically in the centre of the

FURTHER IDEAS

The arrangement on the left is essentially a modern design piece which gives the flower arranger the freedom to express his or her own personality and skill. Use snake bamboo, bear grass and moss: these are very suitable materials for this style of free expression design work. To create the display, complete the arrangement in the candlestick display dish first. Once completed, stand the candlestick base on the foam base and complete the lower section of the arrangement. As you work, ensure that the star shape of the arrangement has five points to give an overall balance without following the corners of the base container (which may not necessarily be square).

arrangement and cut the rest a little shorter. The arrangement will lose its balance if flowers of any type are grouped too heavily in one area. For this reason, as you work, pay close attention to the bands of colour. Alstroemeria has many branches of flowers on one stem, so trim the stem where necessary to suit the placement of the flower in the arrangement. Again, always check the balance and volume of colour.

6 Finally, arrange the roses. The rose is also a round-headed flower and is here used to prettify any gaps. Arrange them as you have the carnations. Avoid too much volume around the base of the upright stem. At this stage, add freesias to correct any gaps in the shape. Turning the arrangement, rework any areas that do not appear to have enough colour, or where the colour is not balanced. Also, take a look from the top of the arrangement to check that the five-pronged star shape looks well balanced, too. Your arrangement is now complete.

Flowers and greenery

- ❧ (1) Spray carnations
- ❧ (2) Leatherleaf
- ❧ (3) Mini gerbera
- ❧ (4) Allium
- ❧ (5) Larkspur
- ❧ (6) Myriocladus
- ❧ (7) Italian ruscus

Materials and equipment

- ❧ Candle stand with cup attachment
- ❧ Floral foam brick
- ❧ Floral tape
- ❧ Frog and floral fix
- ❧ Sharp knife or scissors

DIAGONAL

The diagonal arrangement is formed like a twisted diamond shape. It is a classic design with beautiful lines which can be adapted to a modern interpretation by using different flowers.

METHOD

1 Attach a cup to a candle stand. Wet one-third of a floral foam brick and secure it to the cup using a frog, floral fix and tape. Once in place, you should have approximately 4–5cm (1¾in) of foam showing above the lip of the cup. With this design, unlike the others, angle the foam brick into the cup with one corner facing frontwards, rather than square on. Following the photos, above, and diagram, above right, take some Italian ruscus and create the main arteries of the arrangement, working from 1 to 5. Cut the first stem one and a half times the

size of the candle stand and insert it at 1. Cut a further stem slightly shorter than the first and insert at 2. Cut two further stems to one-third of the length of the first stem and insert them at 3 and 4. Using your own judgement about length, cut a fifth and final stem and insert into the top centre of the foam base to create a line from 1 through to 2.

2 Now turn to the greening. Using the Italian ruscus, create a diagonal frame. The design is a twisted diamond shape, so the top half should be facing to

the right and the bottom half facing to the front and left. Cut two stems to half the size of the first stem at 1 and insert them parallel to the first stem. Likewise, prepare a further two stems and insert at 2. Angle a further stem at 3 towards 1 on the back face of the foam, and angle another at 4 towards 2 on the front of the foam. Take off all unnecessary leaves from the base of the stems of the Italian ruscus as you work to avoid making an unsightly large hole in the foam.

3 Continue to build up the greening with the Italian ruscus, leatherleaf and myriocladus. Each type of greenery has its own usage: Italian ruscus to create the lines, leatherleaf to form the backdrop and myriocladus to fill in. Following the photo, below, insert the flat leatherleaf into the foam, directly behind the Italian ruscus, to provide the backing. This will emphasize the twisted shape

of the arrangement. Take some myriocladus and fill in to emphasize the frame and disguise the foam base. As you can see, once this is completed, the bottom half of the diamond should be twisted and slightly facing the front.

4 Following the photo, above, and accompanying diagram, below, take some stems of larkspur and, keeping the stems to a maximum length, work a diagonal band of colour from top right to bottom left of the arrangement. Larkspur is a line flower and has many blooms in bud on a single stem which lends itself well to emphasizing the outlines and creating movement in the arrangement. Once completed, the twisted diamond shape should be much more apparent.

5 Now take some spray carnations and create another diagonal band of colour with them. Use any flowers in bud with longer stems to create an outline and flowers in bloom with shorter stems to fill in the centre of the arrangement. You will need to place many of the stems in an upward angle from underneath, so alter the angle of the arrangement as you work to ensure that you do not break up the foam unnecessarily and to ensure that your distribution of larkspur and spray carnations is well balanced throughout the centre of the arrangement. If you find that the twist still lacks definition at this stage, replace some of the flowers on the bottom half and place them at a more vertical angle at the back section of the foam base. By following this, you should correct the shape.

6

7a

FURTHER IDEAS

6 Next take some allium, the third main flower in the arrangement. Continuing with the colour banding technique, and following a zigzag formation, place the allium into the arrangement. Place some of the longer stems into the top and bottom halves of the arrangement, ensuring that the stems placed on the bottom half are slightly shorter than those on the top to maintain a sense of balance. Place alliums with as short a stem as possible into the centre of the top of the foam to add to the sense of movement.

7 Finally, take some mini gerbera, the final main flower, and arrange it in a zigzag formation to create an opposite diagonal band of colour. Mini gerbera is a pretty, round-headed flower. To make the most of its sunny character, alter the

angle of each to open up space and create a sense of variety and movement in the arrangement. If you feel the display requires some extra filling in, use stems of spray carnations in bud and larkspur to correct the shape to your satisfaction. Your arrangement is now complete.

7b

To begin this arrangement, first make the basic frame in the shape of a thin rugby ball using twigs and pussy willow bound with gold wire. Use wire to attach two or three further sticks to the bottom of the rugby ball shape which you then insert into the vase to support the arrangement. Spray some flower tubes gold then wire them at random onto the frame. Wrap the frame with trailing asparagus fern to disguise the tubes. Fill the flower tubes with water, then cut some sunflowers short enough to be almost entirely immersed in the tubes and insert them. As you can see in the photo, above, some of the sunflower heads should be inserted facing downwards. Achieve this by using rubber caps on the flower tubes to retain the water. Finally, use leaves of monstera around the mouth of the vase to disguise the inserted sticks and also to give the display extra width.

PART SIX

Natural
Arrangements

Flowers and greenery

- ❦ (1) Freesias
- ❦ (2) Spray carnations
- ❦ (3) Limonium
- ❦ (4) Spray roses
- ❦ (5) Eryngium
- ❦ (6) Sedum
- ❦ (7) Leatherleaf
- ❦ (8) Polygonum

Materials and equipment

- ❦ Basket
- ❦ Plastic dish
- ❦ Floral foam brick
- ❦ Floral fix
- ❦ Floral tape
- ❦ Sharp knife or scissors
- ❦ Optional item: ribbons

COUNTRY GARDEN BASKET

A country garden basket is used for gathering flowers from the garden. The basket is a classic design inspired by the rustic tradition of arranging flowers as if they have just been picked, to fill the home with a fresh, summery fragrance.

METHOD

1 Wet one third of a foam brick and insert it into a plastic dish. Place a floral fix in the centre of the basket and mount the dish on top of it. Secure the dish using floral tape. It is important to be able to see approximately 3–4cm (1½in) of the foam base above the rim of the basket, because the basket is quite flat. Following the photo, above, and the diagram, below left, take some leatherleaf and polygonum and create the main arteries of the arrangement, working from 1 to 4. Cut the first stem to 10cm (4in) longer than the length of the basket which will ensure the arrangement maintains a good balance. Lay this first stem flat along the base of the basket so that the greenery spills over the edge. Cut three further stems to one-third of the length of the first stem and insert them at 2, 3 and 4. Insert stems for 2 and

3 horizontally, one each side of the foam. Insert stems for 1, 2 and 3 at a slightly upward angle from underneath, as if the greenery and flowers are laid in the basket. Insert the stem vertically at 4 one-third in from the right-hand edge on the top of the foam.

2 Next, turn to the greening. Place leatherleaf on the rim of the basket to form a frame between 2, 1 and 3, as if you are creating a half oval shape in

plan. As you can see from the photo of the main arrangement, the flowers in this design are biased towards one end of the basket, at 1.

You will need to incorporate plenty of stems for this part of the arrangement so be aware of leaving some space for the remainder of your flowers. Disguise the foam base with leatherleaf and polygonum. You should also disguise the right-hand side and end of the arrangement, at 2–4–3, with short stems of greenery to disguise the foam and plastic dish. Put aside some stems in case you require them later.

3 Take some stems of polygonum and spray chrysanthemum to create bands of colour within the arrangement. Polygonum, which is also known as snake wood, is a

popular garden flower and has recently become more widely available in the markets. It is a pointed flower which contrasts very well with the round-headed spray chrysanthemums. As you begin to place the flowers, keep an eye on the balance of both volume and colour. Place those with long floral stems into the sides of the foam base, allowing a few to spill slightly over the 2–4–3 outline on the right-hand side of the arrangement.

4 Now turn to the spray roses and sedum, two further main flowers, and place them into the arrangement,

working in a zigzag formation. Place those stems to the centre of the top face of the foam as perfectly vertical as possible, and those along the outline formed by 1 to 4 in a gradually arching shape, from horizontal through vertical to horizontal again on the other side. Again, as you work, keep an eye on the balance of volume and colour to ensure that the spray roses do not overpower the rest of the arrangement. As you place the flat-headed sedum, alter the angle of each slightly to emphasize the sense of movement within the flower arrangement.

5 Next, arrange the freesias and eryngium. Yellow freesias and purple eryngium are common garden flowers which lend a nice contrast to the arrangement. There are a number of varieties of eryngium, each with different-sized heads, and for this arrangement, I have used the smaller, although the larger might be used as a main flower. One of the appealing characteristics of this flower is that its colour does not alter for a long time, even when dried. Arrange both freesias and eryngium throughout the arrangement, ensuring that there is always a good balance between them which will provide plenty of rhythm to the arrangement.

6 Next fill the gaps in the country garden basket with limonium. As you work, turn the arrangement around to check its shape, from all sides. If you have a turntable, it will be much easier. If

119

necessary, correct the outlines with more of the limonium. It is a delicate, small-headed flower, but do be careful not to over-use it or you may affect the essential sense of movement in the arrangement.

7 Finish the arrangement by placing the stems into one end of the display in much the same way as pictured in the photos on the previous page and above. First cut the stems to a length equivalent to two-thirds of the distance between 1 and 4. As you arrange the stems, alter the angle of each to make them look natural, and ensure that they do not stray beyond the width of the basket itself. You can vary the dimensions of your stems, too: use some thicker stems to add variety. Your display should now resemble a bunch of flowers gathered in the basket. Finally, to prettify the arrangement further, you might like to tie a length of ribbon around the stems. How elaborate you would like this to be is up to you. Either keep it simple and rustic by tying a straightforward bow, or secure the stems gently together with one length and then fold a second into a concertina of six loops and tie in the middle with No. 22 wire.

FURTHER IDEAS

This alternative basket can also be filled with plants and flowers from the garden: amaranthus, hydrangea, daisies, rudbeckia and lavender. Another striking addition might be ornamental grasses. To encourage the wild flower stems to drink water, place them overnight in a bucket of water. For grasses in particular, first soak in vinegar and then place in a bucket of water overnight. Your stems will last much longer if you do this. To arrange the display itself, follow the instructions for the Country Garden Basket, with the heads arranged at one end of the basket as though they have just been gathered from the garden.

Index and
Information

ABOUT THE AUTHOR

Taeko Marvelly studied the Ikebana method of flower arranging in Japan where she gained the status of Master. Following further training at the London School of Floristry, she has enjoyed a diverse and prestigious floristry career, including exhibitions at the Chelsea Flower Show and the World Congress of Flowers in Monaco (where she was presented to Princess Grace).

In 1989 she set up the Taeko Marvelly School of Flower Arrangement in both London and Tokyo where students are given a formal training in flower design. Alongside this, she manages a floristry business, The Daisy Chain, commissions for which include displays at the Guildhall, British Museum, the Banqueting House in Whitehall, and a presentation to Princess Anne. She has also contributed to, and been featured by, a number of magazines, both in Japan and the UK.

Now based permanently in London, Taeko works in partnership with her husband, Leonard, and continues successfully to combine all facets of her business ventures.

For further information about commissions or courses, please contact
Taeko Marvelly's School of Flower Arrangement:

UK – 20 Cliffe Road, South Croydon, Surrey CR2 6PQ
Email: tmflower.school@virgin.net

ACKNOWLEDGMENTS

I would like to gratefully acknowledge the following people who have contributed to this book and to the ongoing success of my flower arranging business: my studio assistants Juliet Jones and Robin Chanda, assistant arrangers Gemma Geverink and Rieko Yamagata, assistants Chieko Kurata, Tomoko Watanabe and Keiko Sato, and clerical assistant Miyo McCafferty, my friends Lin and Graham Bonard for the use of their lovely house and garden, Derek Cattani for the wonderful photography featured in this book, Yurie Fujihara for the translation of my text from the original Japanese, Ayako Tanabe for the beautiful Japanese brushwork, and finally my partner, Leonard Marvelly for his invaluable help with the English language!

INDEX

UPHOLSTERY

TOYMAKING

DOLLS' HOUSES AND MINIATURES

CRAFTS

GARDENING

Auriculas for Everyone: How to Grow and Show Perfect Plants		Growing Cacti and Other Succulents in the Garden	Shirley-Anne Bell
	Mary Robinson	Hardy Perennials: A Beginner's Guide	Eric Sawford
Beginners' Guide to Herb Gardening	Yvonne Cuthbertson	Hedges: Creating Screens and Edges	Averil Bedrich
Beginners' Guide to Water Gardening	Graham Clarke	The Living Tropical Greenhouse: Creating a Haven for Butterflies	
Bird Boxes and Feeders for the Garden	Dave Mackenzie		John & Maureen Tampion
The Birdwatcher's Garden	Hazel & Pamela Johnson	Marginal Plants	Bernard Sleeman
Broad-Leaved Evergreens	Stephen G. Haw	Orchids are Easy: A Beginner's Guide to their Care and Cultivation	
Companions to Clematis: Growing Clematis with Other Plants			Tom Gilland
	Marigold Badcock	Plant Alert: A Garden Guide for Parents	Catherine Collins
Creating Contrast with Dark Plants	Freya Martin	Planting Plans for Your Garden	Jenny Shukman
Creating Small Habitats for Wildlife in your Garden	Josie Briggs	Plants that Span the Seasons	Roger Wilson
Exotics are Easy	GMC Publications	Sink and Container Gardening Using Dwarf Hardy Plants	Chris & Valerie Wheeler
Gardening with Hebes	Chris & Valerie Wheeler		
Gardening with Wild Plants	Julian Slatcher	The Successful Conservatory and Growing Exotic Plants	Joan Phelan
Growing Cacti and Other Succulents in the Conservatory and Indoors		Tropical Garden Style with Hardy Plants	Alan Hemsley
	Shirley-Anne Bell	Water Garden Projects: From Groundwork to Planting	Roger Sweetinburgh

ART TECHNIQUES

Oil Paintings from your Garden: A Guide for Beginners	Rachel Shirley

PHOTOGRAPHY

Close-Up on Insects	Robert Thompson	Outdoor Photography Portfolio	GMC Publications
An Essential Guide to Bird Photography	Steve Young	Photographing Fungi in the Field	George McCarthy
Field Guide to Landscape Photography	Peter Watson	Photography for the Naturalist	Mark Lucock
How to Photograph Pets	Nick Ridley	Viewpoints from Outdoor Photography	GMC Publications
LIfe in the Wild: A Photographer's Year	Andy Rouse	Where and How to Photograph Wildlife	Peter Evans
Light in the Landscape: A Photographer's Year	Peter Watson		

VIDEOS

Drop-in and Pinstuffed Seats	David James	Twists and Advanced Turning	Dennis White
Stuffover Upholstery	David James	Sharpening the Professional Way	Jim Kingshott
Elliptical Turning	David Springett	Sharpening Turning & Carving Tools	Jim Kingshott
Woodturning Wizardry	David Springett	Bowl Turning	John Jordan
Turning Between Centres: The Basics	Dennis White	Hollow Turning	John Jordan
Turning Bowls	Dennis White	Woodturning: A Foundation Course	Keith Rowley
Boxes, Goblets and Screw Threads	Dennis White	Carving a Figure: The Female Form	Ray Gonzalez
Novelties and Projects	Dennis White	The Router: A Beginner's Guide	Alan Goodsell
Classic Profiles	Dennis White	The Scroll Saw: A Beginner's Guide	John Burke

MAGAZINES

WOODTURNING ◆ WOODCARVING ◆ FURNITURE & CABINETMAKING
THE ROUTER ◆ NEW WOODWORKING ◆ THE DOLLS' HOUSE MAGAZINE
◆ OUTDOOR PHOTOGRAPHY ◆ BLACK & WHITE PHOTOGRAPHY
MACHINE KNITTING NEWS ◆ BusinessMatters

The above represents a full list of all titles currently published or scheduled to be published.
All are available direct from the Publishers or through bookshops, newsagents and specialist retailers.
To place an order, or to obtain a complete catalogue, contact:

GMC Publications, 166 High Street, Lewes, East Sussex BN7 1XU United Kingdom
Tel: 01273 488005 Fax: 01273 478606
E-mail: pubs@thegmcgroup.com

Orders by credit card are accepted

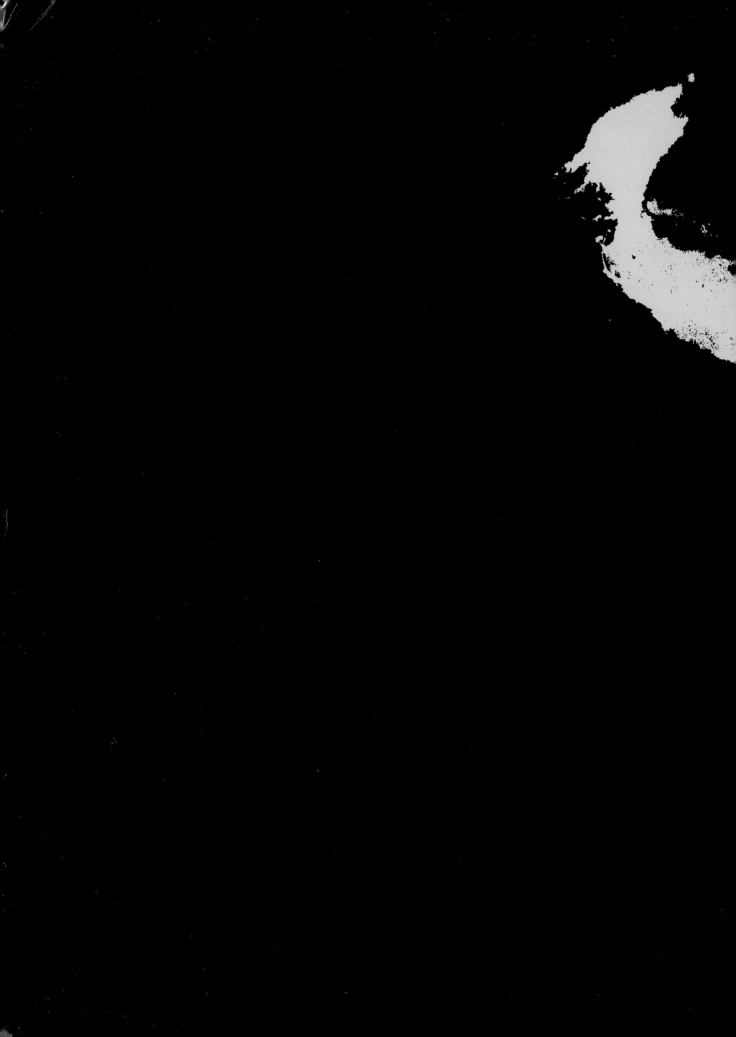